Special Education Law Annual Review 2020

Special Education Law, Policy, and Practice

Series Editors: Mitchell L. Yell, PhD, University of South Carolina
David F. Bateman, PhD, Shippensburg University

The Special Education Law, Policy, and Practice series highlights current trends and legal issues in the education of students with disabilities. The books in this series link legal requirements with evidence-based instruction and highlight practical applications for working with students with disabilities. The titles in the Special Education Law, Policy, and Practices series are designed not only to be required textbooks for general education and special education preservice teacher education programs but also for practicing teachers, education administrators, principals, school counselors, school psychologists, parents, and others interested in improving the lives of students with disabilities. The Special Education Law, Policy, and Practice series is committed to research-based practices working to provide appropriate and meaningful educational programming for students with disabilities and their families.

Titles in Series

The Essentials of Special Education Law
by Andrew M. Markelz and David F. Bateman

Special Education Law Annual Review 2020
by David F. Bateman, Mitchell L. Yell, and Kevin P. Brady

Developing Educationally Meaningful and Legally Sound IEPs
by Mitchell L. Yell, David F. Bateman, and James G. Shriner

Sexuality Education for Students with Disabilities
by Thomas C. Gibbon, Elizabeth Harkins Monaco, and David F. Bateman

Creating Positive Elementary Classrooms: Preventing Behavior Challenges to Promote Learning
by Stephen W. Smith and Mitchell L. Yell

Special Education Law Annual Review 2020

David F. Bateman
Shippensburg University

Mitchell L. Yell
University of South Carolina

Kevin P. Brady
University of Arkansas

ROWMAN & LITTLEFIELD
Lanham • Boulder • New York • London

Acquisitions Editor: Mark Kerr
Assistant Editor: Courtney Packard
Sales and Marketing Inquiries: textbooks@rowman.com

Credits and acknowledgments for material borrowed from other sources, and reproduced with permission, appear on the appropriate pages within the text.

Published by Rowman & Littlefield
An imprint of The Rowman & Littlefield Publishing Group, Inc.
4501 Forbes Boulevard, Suite 200, Lanham, Maryland 20706
www.rowman.com

86-90 Paul Street, London EC2A 4NE

Copyright © 2022 by The Rowman & Littlefield Publishing Group, Inc.

All rights reserved. No part of this book may be reproduced in any form or by any electronic or mechanical means, including information storage and retrieval systems, without written permission from the publisher, except by a reviewer who may quote passages in a review.

British Library Cataloguing in Publication Information Available

Library of Congress ISSN Pending

Disclaimer

The information in the *Special Education Law Annual* is not legal advice, nor should it replace legal advice. Information in the annual may be affected by state statutes, regulations, and local or district policies and practices. In incidences involving potentially legal situations, the services of a licensed attorney should be secured.

Contents

Introduction xi

1 The US Department of Education, the IDEA, and Section 504 1

2 Policy Letters from the US Department of Education 3

3 A Primer on Dispute Resolution Under the IDEA and Section 504 61

4 Researching Special Education Law Online 69

5 Topics Covered by US Courts of Appeals in 2020 75

6 Case Summaries by Circuit 83

Glossary of Legal Terms 169
References 177
Index 179

Detailed Contents

Introduction xi

1 The US Department of Education, the IDEA, and Section 504   1

2 Policy Letters from the US Department of Education   3
2.1 Dear Colleague Letters 4
2.2 Guidance from OSEP 11

3 A Primer on Dispute Resolution Under the IDEA and Section 504   61
3.1 Dispute Resolution 61
3.2 Special Education Disputes in the Federal Court System 63
3.3 Published and Unpublished Decisions 68

4 Researching Special Education Law Online   69

5 Topics Covered by US Courts of Appeals in 2020   75
5.1 504 75
5.2 Abuse 75
5.3 Administration Remedies 75
5.4 Attorney's Fees 76
5.5 Child Find 76
5.6 Compensatory Education 76
5.7 Discrimination 76
5.8 Eligibility 77
5.9 Enrollment 77
5.10 Escrow Accounts 77
5.11 Evaluation 77
5.12 FAPE 77
5.13 First Amendment 78
5.14 Functional Behavior Assessment 78
5.15 Harassment 78
5.16 Independent Educational Evaluation 78

5.17 Individualized Education Program (IEP)-FAPE   78
5.18 Jurisdiction   78
5.19 Least Restrictive Environment   79
5.20 Literacy   79
5.21 Mootness   79
5.22 Noncustodial Parents   79
5.23 Paraprofessionals   79
5.24 Placement   79
5.25 Procedural Violations   79
5.26 *Pro se*   79
5.27 Residency   80
5.28 Residential Placement   80
5.29 Standard for Review   80
5.30 Statute of Limitations   80
5.31 Stay Put   80
5.32 Transportation   81
5.33 Tuition Reimbursement   81

6 Case Summaries by Circuit   83

6.1 Case Summaries from the US Court of Appeals, Second Circuit   88
6.2 Case Summaries from the US Court of Appeals, Third Circuit   98
6.3 Case Summaries from the US Court of Appeals, Fourth Circuit   109
6.4 Case Summaries from the US Court of Appeals, Fifth Circuit   111
6.5 Case Summaries from the US Court of Appeals, Sixth Circuit   126
6.6 Case Summaries from the US Court of Appeals, Eighth Circuit   133
6.7 Case Summaries from the US Court of Appeals, Ninth Circuit   138
6.8 Case Summaries from the US Court of Appeals, Tenth Circuit   158
6.9 Case Summaries from the US Court of Appeals, Eleventh Circuit   163
6.10 Case Summaries from the US Court of Appeals, DC Circuit   164

Glossary of Legal Terms   169
References   177
Index   179

Introduction

The global COVID-19 pandemic of 2020 changed the way educators provide instruction and the way they interact with students. Although the education of all students was affected by the pandemic, the education of students with disabilities has been particularly problematic. This is because students with disabilities who are eligible under the Individuals with Disabilities Education Act (IDEA) and Section 504 have a federal right to receive a free appropriate public education (FAPE). The US Department of Education has made clear that the pandemic did not relieve school districts of their responsibility to provide FAPE.

All students have no doubt regressed to some degree during the closure of public schools during the pandemic; unfortunately, students with disabilities who have serious educational needs requiring intensive instruction have most likely regressed significantly and will have difficulty recouping these losses. In addition to these problems, students with poor or no Internet access may not have been able to access the virtual instruction offered by their local school district. Moreover, school personnel may not have had information regarding their students' educational and functional progress over the past year. This summary of all the major special education appellate court cases from 2020 does not include any cases that addressed the COVID-19 pandemic. Readers may find this surprising; however, the cases we review are from the US circuit courts of appeals, and cases regarding the COVID-19 pandemic will take a while to reach that level.

For a case to reach a US circuit court of appeals, it usually goes through a due process hearing and then through appeals to a US district court, perhaps multiple appeals. The process may take several years. There may be cases involving the education that students with disabilities received during the COVID-19 pandemic in the US circuit courts beginning now. The pace of appeals is often slow. Due process hearings at the first tier are supposed to be held with a decision reached within 45 days of the hearing request. No such speed exists once the hearing is appealed up the judicial system. We believe these pandemic cases will be coming.

This edition of the annual review does not contain any cases from the US Supreme Court. We would have reviewed any case the Supreme Court ruled on, but there have been no decisions from that court since the *Endrew F. v. Douglas County School District* ruling in March 2017. There have been 12 special education rulings from the US Supreme Court, 13 counting a case that ended in a tie vote (4-4) and thus no ruling, in the 46 years from the passage of the IDEA. Obviously, there are not many Supreme Court cases heard on special education, and we will report on them when they occur.

In this annual edition we include copies of all policy statements, Dear Colleague Letters, and frequently-asked-questions (FAQ) documents from the

US Department of Education related to the education of students with disabilities. We review rulings related to the IDEA and Section 504 from US courts of appeals for 2020, presented by circuit. The list of cases was developed by analyzing all circuit cases in the LRP and Westlaw Databases for special education for the calendar year 2020. The summaries we present do not address all points covered in a case. If a case has been published, we reference the citation for the reader who would like to review the complete case. We also provide a primer on the IDEA dispute resolution process, a guide on researching cases online, and lists of websites for follow-up research related to online special education law. This annual edition is a comprehensive summary of 2020 appellate court cases in special education and comprises important information and principles for all those who work closely with students with disabilities in K–12 educational settings.

CHAPTER 1

The US Department of Education, the IDEA, and Section 504

The US Department of Education is comprised of several offices, three of which are especially crucial to the education of children and youth with disabilities. One of these offices is the Office of Special Education and Related Services (OSERS). The mission of OSERS is "to improve early childhood, educational, and employment outcomes and raise expectations for all people with disabilities, their families, their communities, and the nation" (OSERS Website, p. 1). The Office of Special Education Programs (OSEP) is located within OSERS. The OSEP is dedicated to improving results for infants, toddlers, children, and youth with disabilities ages birth through 21 by providing leadership and financial support to assist states and local districts through the IDEA. Both OSERS and OSEP provide leadership, enforcement, and fiscal resources to assist states and local school districts to educate students with disabilities.

Another office within the US Department of Education is the Office of Civil Rights (OCR). "The mission of the Office for Civil Rights is to ensure equal access to education and to promote educational excellence throughout the nation through vigorous enforcement of civil rights" (OCR Website, p. 1). The OCR enforces several civil rights laws that prohibit discrimination against persons with disabilities, including Section 504 of the Rehabilitation Act, which prohibits discrimination against persons with disabilities in entities receiving federal financial assistance, and Title II of the Americans with Disabilities Act, which prohibits discrimination against persons with disabilities by public entities whether or not they receive federal funding.

All three of these offices develop, communicate, and disseminate federal policy interpretations through policy letters, guidance documents, question-and-answer documents, and memos that address special education and children and youth with disabilities. The letters issued by these offices may be in the form of answers to queries by individuals (e.g., Letter to ___) or open letters called Dear Colleague Letters. The purpose of these documents is to explain or interpret federal law and regulations. Although these guidance documents are nonbinding and do not have the force of law, they may be cited in hearings or court cases because the guidance has some legal authority. Moreover, it is important to pay attention to these guidance documents because they present helpful explanations of existing laws and regulations and provide information regarding how these administrative agencies will enforce the existing laws and regulations.

During 2020, OSERS, OSEP, and OCR issued several policy statements regarding children and youth with disabilities. Although any federal agency (e.g., US Department of Justice) may issue administrative guidance, we are most concerned with guidance from the US Department of Education, most specifically letters issued by OSERS, OSEP, and OCR. These guidance documents are very important to special education administrators and teachers, related service providers, and parents of children and youth with disabilities because they provide official guidance and clarification on the implementation of the IDEA and Section 504. The Department of Education maintains websites that collect the letters of guidance and other policy documents. These guidance documents from OSEP and OSERS can be found at https://www2.ed.gov/policy/speced/guid/idea/memosdcltrs/index.html. Guidance documents from OCR can be found in the OCR Reading Room at https://www2.ed.gov/about/offices/list/ocr/frontpage/faq/readingroom.html.

CHAPTER 2

Policy Letters from the US Department of Education

2.1	**Dear Colleague Letters**	4
	2.1.1 June 8, 2020 Part B money and payment of hearing officers	4
	2.1.2 July 31, 2020 Confidentiality and mediation	8
2.2	**Guidance from OSEP**	11
	2.2.1 March 2020 Questions and answers on providing services to children with disabilities during the 2020 COVID-19 outbreak	11
	2.2.2 March 21, 2020 Supplemental fact sheet addressing the risk of COVID-19 in preschools, elementary schools, and secondary schools while serving children with disabilities	18
	2.2.3 June 9, 2020 Waiver on Alternate Assessment Aligned with Alternate Academic Achievement Standards (AA-AAAS)	23
	2.2.4 June 22, 2020 IDEA Part B Resolution Process	28
	2.2.5 June 22, 2020 IDEA Part C Resolution Process	32
	2.2.6 June 25, 2020 IDEA Part B Use of Funds	36
	2.2.7 June 25, 2020 IDEA Part C Use of Funds	41
	2.2.8 June 26, 2020 Flexibility of IDEA Part B Fiscal Requirements	45
	2.2.9 June 30, 2020 IDEA Part B Procedural Safeguards	49
	2.2.10 June 30, 2020 IDEA Part C Procedural Safeguards	53
	2.2.11 July 6, 2020 Initial Evaluations and Timelines Part C	57

2.1.1

UNITED STATES DEPARTMENT OF EDUCATION
OFFICE OF SPECIAL EDUCATION AND REHABILITATIVE SERVICES

June 8, 2020

Dear XXXXXXXXX:

This letter addresses your February 20, 2020, electronic correspondence to me regarding the use of Individuals with Disabilities Education Act (IDEA) Part B funds to pay hearing officers to conduct due process hearings under IDEA. Specifically, you ask whether it is permissible for States to use IDEA Part B funds for this purpose. We regret the delay in responding.

We note that Section 607(d) of IDEA prohibits the Secretary from issuing policy letters or other statements that establish a rule that is required for compliance with, and eligibility under, IDEA without following the rulemaking requirements of Section 553 of the Administrative Procedure Act. Therefore, based on the requirements of IDEA Section 607(e), this response is provided as informal guidance and is not legally binding. This response represents an interpretation by the U.S. Department of Education (Department) of the requirements of IDEA in the context of the specific facts presented and does not establish a policy or rule that would apply in all circumstances.

The answer to your question requires an examination of the requirements that apply to Federal grants under the Uniform Administrative Requirements, Cost Principles, and Audit Requirements for Federal Awards (hereafter, Uniform Guidance) as well as IDEA and its implementing regulations.

Uniform Guidance: Allowability of Costs Charged to Federal Awards

Subpart E of 2 C.F.R Part 200, Cost Principles of the Uniform Guidance, sets out general criteria that must be met for costs to be allowable under Federal awards. To charge a cost to a Federal award, among other factors, it must be necessary and reasonable for the performance of the Federal award and be allocable to the Federal grant. 2 C.F.R. § 200.403.

A cost is reasonable if, in its nature and amount, it does not exceed that which would be incurred by a prudent person under the circumstances prevailing at the time the decision was made to incur the cost. The reasonableness of a given cost is determined by applying the considerations in 2 C.F.R. § 200.404, including whether the cost is of a type generally recognized as ordinary and necessary for the operation of the non-Federal entity or the proper and efficient performance of the Federal award. A cost is allocable to a particular Federal award or other cost objective if the goods or services involved are chargeable or assignable to the Federal award or cost objective in accordance with the relative benefits received. The requirements for meeting this standard are set forth in 2 C.F.R. § 200.405.

The Uniform Guidance, at 2 C.F.R. §§ 200.420–200.475, sets out "General Provisions for Selected Items of Cost." Among the items included are "[c]osts of professional and consultant services rendered by persons who are members of a particular profession or possess a special skill, and who are not officers or employees of the non-Federal entity," which are allowable, subject to certain conditions. 2 C.F.R. § 200.459(a). The regulation sets out the relevant factors in determining the allowability of such costs. 2 C.F.R. § 200.459(b).

Part B of IDEA: Ensuring the Opportunity for an Impartial Due Process Hearing

The Department makes grants to States to assist them in providing special education and related services to children with disabilities in accordance with Part B of IDEA. 20 U.S.C. 1411(a)(1); 34 C.F.R. § 300.700(a). A portion of the State's allocation may be reserved by the State for the purpose of administering Part B of IDEA. 20 U.S.C. 1411(e)(1); 34 C.F.R. § 300.704(a).

In its application for IDEA Part B funds, pursuant to Assurance 6, a State must assure that it has policies and procedures in place to ensure children with disabilities and their parents are afforded the procedural safeguards required by 34 C.F.R. §§ 300.500 through 300.536, and in accordance with 20 U.S.C. 1412(a)(6) and 34 C.F.R. § 300.121. These policies and procedures include ensuring that whenever a due process complaint is received under 34 C.F.R. §§ 300.507 or 300.532, the parents and the local educational agency (LEA) involved in the dispute have an opportunity for an impartial due process hearing, consistent with the procedures in 34 C.F.R. §§ 300.507, 300.508, and 300.510. 34 C.F.R. § 300.511(a).

In a one-tier due process system, the State educational agency (SEA) conducts the impartial due process hearing. 34 C.F.R. § 300.511(b). Under 34 C.F.R. § 300.511(c)(1)(i)–(ii), a hearing officer may not be an employee of the SEA or the LEA that is involved in the education or care of the child and must have no personal or professional interest that conflicts with the person's objectivity at the hearing. Further, an individual who otherwise qualifies as a hearing officer is not an employee of the SEA or the LEA that is responsible for conducting the hearing solely because he or she is paid by the agency to serve as a hearing officer. 34 C.F.R. § 300.511(c)(2). Thus, it is not uncommon for the SEA to contract with another entity to conduct impartial due process hearings. Because the State is required to ensure that parents and LEAs have an opportunity for an impartial due process hearing, costs of paying hearing officers that conduct due process hearings in a one-tier State where the SEA is responsible for conducting the hearing, are allocable to a State's IDEA Part B grant award, subject to the Uniform Guidance cost principles described above, and a portion of the Part B funds reserved for State administration in 34 C.F.R. § 300.704(a) may be used for this purpose.

While your letter does not ask about whether LEAs can use their Part B allocations to pay hearing officers, we also wish to clarify that the expenditure of an LEA's Part B allocation for this purpose is also permissible for the reasons described above. In a two-tier due process system, the public agency directly responsible for the education of the child conducts the impartial due process hearing. 34 C.F.R. § 300.511(b). As previously noted by the Department, nothing in Part B would prevent an LEA from using its Part B allocation for the cost of conducting these hearings, "so long as the expenditures meet the other applicable requirements under the Act and regulations." Assistance to States for the Education of Children with Disabilities and Preschool Grants for Children with Disabilities, Final Rule, Analysis of Comments and Changes, 71 Fed. Reg. 46540, 46624 (Aug. 14, 2006). Just as in a one-tier due process system where the cost of the hearing officer can be paid for with IDEA Part B funds reserved for State administration, the costs of the hearing officers are allocable to the LEA's IDEA

Part B subgrant award, consistent with the Uniform Guidance cost principles summarized above and at 34 C.F.R. § 300.202(a)(1).

If you have any further questions, please do not hesitate to contact Rebecca Walawender of my staff at 202-245-7399 or by email at Rebecca.Walawender@ed.gov.

Sincerely, /s/
Laurie VanderPloeg
Director
Office of Special Education Programs

2.1.2

UNITED STATES DEPARTMENT OF EDUCATION
OFFICE OF SPECIAL EDUCATION AND REHABILITATIVE SERVICES

July 31, 2020

Dear XXXXXXXXXXX:

This letter addresses your November 8, 2019, electronic mail (email) correspondence to Rebecca Walawender, a member of my staff in the U.S. Department of Education (Department), Office of Special Education Programs (OSEP). In that correspondence you shared your communications with an official of the Texas Education Agency (TEA) concerning whether a parent may be required to sign a confidentiality agreement in order to participate in mediation under Part B of the Individuals with Disabilities Education Act (IDEA). In your communication with TEA, a TEA official informed you that although a confidentiality pledge is not required, a school district may withdraw from the mediation process if a parent refuses to sign such an agreement. You contacted OSEP to request clarification regarding whether a public agency, in this case a local educational agency, may condition its participation in mediation on a parent's agreement to sign a confidentiality pledge. We regret the delay in responding.

We note that section 607(d) of IDEA prohibits the Secretary from issuing policy letters or other statements that establish a rule that is required for compliance with, and eligibility under, IDEA without following the rulemaking requirements of section 553 of the Administrative Procedure Act. Therefore, based on the requirements of IDEA section 607(e), this response is provided as informal guidance and is not legally binding. This response represents an interpretation by the Department of the requirements of IDEA in the context of the specific facts presented and does not establish a policy or rule that would apply in all circumstances.

Under IDEA, discussions that occur during mediation sessions must remain confidential. 34 C.F.R. § 300.506(b)(6) and (8). Therefore, a parent's or public agency's participation in the mediation process may not be conditioned on the party's agreement to sign a confidentiality pledge. IDEA and its implementing regulations require public agencies to establish and implement procedures to allow parties to resolve disputes involving any matter under IDEA and its implementing regulations, including matters arising prior to the filing of a due process complaint, through a mediation process. 20 U.S.C. 1415(e)(1) and 34 C.F.R. § 300.506(a). The public agency must ensure, among other requirements, that the mediation process is voluntary on the part of the parties. 34 C.F.R. § 300.506(b)(1)(i). Additionally, mediation may not be used to deny or delay a parent's right to a hearing on the parent's due process complaint, or to deny any other rights afforded under Part B of IDEA. 34 C.F.R. § 300.506(b)(1)(ii). The goal of mediation is for the parties to resolve the dispute and execute a legally binding written agreement reflecting that resolution.

In its July 2013 "Questions and Answers on IDEA Part B Dispute Resolution Procedures" (available at https://sites.ed.gov/idea/idea-files/osep-memo-and-qa-on-dispute-resolution/), OSEP responded to an inquiry asking whether parties to the mediation process may be required to sign a confidentiality pledge or agreement. That question and answer, which is restated below, remains the Department's position:

Question A-26: May parties to the mediation process be required to sign a confidentiality pledge or agreement prior to, or as a precondition, to the commencement of the mediation process?

Answer: No. In the Notice of Proposed Rulemaking implementing the IDEA Amendments of 2004, the Department included a provision that would have required parties to a mediation to sign a confidentiality pledge, without regard to whether the mediation ultimately resolved the dispute. 70 FR 35870 (June 21, 2005). This proposed provision was based on Note 208 of Conf. Rpt. (Conference Report) No. 108–779, p. 216 (2004). However, the Department decided to remove this proposed provision when the final Part B regulations were published in 2006 based on the statutory requirement in section 615(e)(2)(G) that discussions that occur during the mediation process must remain confidential and may not be used as evidence in any subsequent due process hearing or civil proceeding. 71 FR 46696 (August 14, 2006).

Additionally, if the parties resolve a dispute through the mediation process, as noted above, 34 C.F.R. § 300.506(b)(6)(i) requires that the legally binding written agreement contain a statement that all discussions that occurred during the mediation process will remain confidential and may not be used as evidence in any subsequent due process hearing or civil proceeding. 34 C.F.R. § 300.506(b)(6)(i). This is so even if the parties do not enter into a mediation agreement. However, nothing in these regulations is intended to prevent States from allowing parties to sign a confidentiality pledge to ensure that discussions during the mediation process remain confidential, irrespective of whether the mediation results in a legally binding written agreement resolving the dispute. 71 FR 46696 (August 14, 2006).

The Department's position that States may not require parties to sign a confidentiality pledge is reinforced by the Department's decision in the 2006 final Part B regulations to remove a proposed regulation that would have required parties to sign a confidentiality pledge. 71 Fed. Reg. at 46696 (Aug. 14, 2006). In addition to the provision that must be included in a mediation agreement, 34 C.F.R. § 300.506(b)(8) also provides that discussions that occur during the mediation process must be confidential and may not be used as evidence in any subsequent due process hearing or civil proceeding of any Federal court or State court of a State receiving assistance under Part B of IDEA. Accordingly, the requirement that discussions that occur during mediation remain confidential is fully applicable regardless of whether the parties sign a separate confidentiality pledge or agreement prior to commencing the mediation process. We recognize that mediation is voluntary on the part of the parties, but it is impermissible under IDEA for a public agency to condition a parent's participation in mediation on the parent's signing a confidentiality pledge. While nothing in IDEA is intended to prevent States from allowing parties to sign a confidentiality pledge, public agencies may not condition their participation in mediation on such an agreement, because such a requirement is counter to the voluntary nature of the mediation process.

By copy of this letter, we are notifying TEA of your inquiry and our response. OSEP staff will follow up separately with TEA officials regarding this matter.

If you have any further questions, please do not hesitate to contact Ms. Walawender at 202-245-7399 or by email at Rebecca.Walawender@ed.gov.

Sincerely, /s/
Laurie VanderPloeg
Director
Office of Special Education Program
cc: Justin Porter, Texas Education Agency

2.2.1

QUESTIONS AND ANSWERS ON PROVIDING SERVICES TO CHILDREN WITH DISABILITIES DURING THE CORONAVIRUS DISEASE 2019 OUTBREAK MARCH 2020

The Centers for Disease Control and Prevention (CDC) is responding to an outbreak of respiratory disease caused by a new coronavirus named coronavirus disease 2019 (COVID-19).

The CDC has issued interim guidance to help administrators of public and private childcare programs and K–12 schools plan for and prevent the spread of COVID-19 among students and staff. *See* Interim Guidance for Administrators of US Childcare Programs and K–12 Schools to Plan, Prepare, and Respond to Coronavirus Disease 2019 available at https://www.cdc.gov/coronavirus/2019-ncov/specific-groups/guidance-for-schools.html.

This Questions and Answers document outlines states' responsibilities to infants, toddlers, and children with disabilities and their families, and to the staff serving these children. During an outbreak of COVID-19, local educational agencies (LEAs) and early intervention service (EIS) programs will need to collaborate with their state educational agency (SEA), Bureau of Indian Education (BIE), or local public health department, as appropriate, to address questions about how, what, and when services should be provided to children with disabilities.

It does not create or confer any rights for or on any person. This Q & A document does not impose any additional requirements beyond those included in applicable law and regulations. The responses presented in this document generally constitute informal guidance representing the interpretation of the Department of the applicable statutory or regulatory requirements in the context of the specific facts presented here and are not legally binding. The Q & As in this document are not intended to be a replacement for careful study of the Individuals with Disabilities Education Act (IDEA), Section 504 of the Rehabilitation Act of 1973 (Section 504), Title II of the Americans with Disabilities Act of 1990 (Title II), and their implementing regulations. The IDEA, its implementing regulations, and other important documents related to the IDEA can be found at http://sites.ed.gov/idea. For more information on the requirements of Section 504 and Title II, and their implementing regulations, please consult https://www2.ed.gov/policy/rights/guid/ocr/disabilityoverview.html.

This document does not address when to dismiss a child or close a school or Part C state lead agency because school officials should work with their local health departments to make those decisions. School personnel and Part C EIS programs and providers, however, may consult the Centers for Disease Control and Prevention's (CDC's) guidance for recommendations regarding social distancing and school closure. The CDC's Web site contains information addressing both state and local public health officials and school administrators for school (K–12) responses to COVID-19 and resources for child care and early childhood programs. These documents, along with other recommendations, may be accessed at https://www.cdc.gov/coronavirus/2019-ncov/community/index.html.

A. Implementing Part B of the IDEA and Section 504 during a COVID-19 outbreak

Question A-1: Is an LEA required to continue to provide a free appropriate public education (FAPE) to students with disabilities during a school closure caused by a COVID-19 outbreak?

Answer: The IDEA, Section 504, and Title II of the ADA do not specifically address a situation in which elementary and secondary schools are closed for an extended period of time (generally more than 10 consecutive days) because of exceptional circumstances, such as an outbreak of a particular disease.

If an LEA closes its schools to slow or stop the spread of COVID-19, and does not provide any educational services to the general student population, then an LEA would not be required to provide services to students with disabilities during that same period of time. Once school resumes, the LEA must make every effort to provide special education and related services to the child in accordance with the child's individualized education program (IEP) or, for students entitled to FAPE under Section 504, consistent with a plan developed to meet the requirements of Section 504. The Department understands there may be exceptional circumstances that could affect how a particular service is provided. In addition, an IEP Team and, as appropriate to an individual student with a disability, the personnel responsible for ensuring FAPE to a student for the purposes of Section 504, would be required to make an individualized determination as to whether compensatory services are needed under applicable standards and requirements.

If an LEA continues to provide educational opportunities to the general student population during a school closure, the school must ensure that students with disabilities also have equal access to the same opportunities, including the provision of FAPE. (34 CFR §§ 104.4, 104.33 (Section 504) and 28 CFR § 35.130 (Title II of the ADA)). SEAs, LEAs, and schools must ensure that, to the greatest extent possible, each student with a disability can be provided the special education and related services identified in the student's IEP developed under IDEA, or a plan developed under Section 504. (34 CFR §§ 300.101 and 300.201 (IDEA), and 34 CFR § 104.33 (Section 504)).

Question A-2: Must an LEA provide special education and related services to a child with a disability who is absent for an extended period of time because the child is infected with COVID-19, while the schools remain open?

Answer: Yes. It has long been the Department's position that when a child with a disability is classified as needing homebound instruction because of a medical problem, as ordered by a physician, and is home for an extended period of time (generally more than 10 consecutive school days), an individualized education program (IEP) meeting is necessary to change the child's placement and the contents of the child's IEP, if warranted. Further, if the IEP goals will remain the same and only the time in special education will change, then the IEP Team may add an amendment to the IEP stating specifically the amount of time to be spent in special education. If a child with a disability is absent for an extended period of time because of a COVID-19 infection and the school remains open, then the IEP Team must determine whether the child is available for instruction and could benefit from homebound services such as online or virtual instruction, instructional telephone calls, and other curriculum-based instructional activities, to the extent available. In so doing, school personnel should follow appropriate health guidelines to assess and address the risk of transmission in the provision of such services. The Department understands there may be exceptional circumstances that could affect how a particular service is provided.

If a child does not receive services after an extended period of time, a school must make an individualized determination whether and to what extent compensatory services may be needed, consistent with applicable requirements, including to make up for any skills that may have been lost.

Question A-3: What services must an LEA provide if a public school for children with disabilities is selectively closed due to the possibility of severe complications from a COVID-19 outbreak?

Answer: If a public school for children with disabilities is closed solely because the children are at high risk of severe illness and death, the LEA must determine whether each dismissed child could benefit from online or virtual instruction, instructional telephone calls, and other curriculum-based instructional activities, to the extent available. In so doing, school personnel should follow appropriate health guidelines to assess and address the risk of transmission in the provision of such services. The Department understands there may be exceptional circumstances that could affect how a particular service is provided.

If a child does not receive services during a closure, a child's IEP team (or appropriate personnel under Section 504) must make an individualized determination whether and to what extent compensatory services may be needed, consistent with applicable requirements, including to make up for any skills that may have been lost.

Question A-4: If a child with a disability at high risk of severe medical complications is excluded from school during an outbreak of COVID-19 and the child's school remains open, is the exclusion considered a change in educational placement subject to the protections of 34 CFR §§ 300.115 and 300.116 and 34 CFR §§ 104.35 and 104.36?

Answer: If the exclusion is a temporary emergency measure (generally 10 consecutive school days or less), the provision of services such as online or virtual instruction, instructional telephone calls, and other curriculum-based instructional activities, to the extent available, is not considered a change in placement. During this time period, a child's parent or other IEP team member may request an IEP meeting to discuss the potential need for services if the exclusion is likely to be of long duration (generally more than 10 consecutive school days). For long-term exclusions, an LEA must consider placement decisions under the IDEA's procedural protections of 34 CFR §§ 300.115–300.116, regarding the continuum of alternative placements and the determination of placements.

Under 34 CFR § 300.116, a change in placement decision must be made by a group of persons, including the parents and other persons knowledgeable about the child and the placement options. If the placement group determines that the child meets established high-risk criteria and, due to safety and health concerns, the child's needs could be met through homebound instruction, then under 34 CFR §300.503(a)(1), the public agency must issue a prior written notice proposing the change in placement. A parent who disagrees with this prior written notice retains all of the due process rights included in 34 CFR §§ 300.500–300.520.

For children with disabilities protected by Section 504 who are dismissed from school during an outbreak of COVID-19 because they are at high risk for health complications, compliance with the procedures described above and completion of any necessary evaluations of the child satisfy the evaluation, placement, and procedural requirements of 34 CFR §§ 104.35 and 104.36. The decision to dismiss a child based on his or her high risk for medical complications must be based on the individual needs of the child and not on perceptions of the child's needs based merely on stereotypes or generalizations regarding his or her disability.

Question A-5: May an IEP Team consider a distance learning plan in a child's IEP as a contingency plan in the event of a COVID-19 outbreak that requires the school's closure?

Answer: Yes. IEP teams may, but are not required to, include distance learning plans in a child's IEP that could be triggered and implemented during a selective closure due to a COVID-19 outbreak. Such contingent provisions may include the provision of special education and related services at an alternate location or the provision of online or virtual instruction, instructional telephone calls, and other curriculum-based instructional activities, and may identify which special education and related services, if any, could be provided at the child's home.

Creating a contingency plan before a COVID-19 outbreak occurs gives the child's service providers and the child's parents an opportunity to reach agreement as to what circumstances would trigger the use of the child's distance learning plan and the services that would be provided during the dismissal.

Question A-6: What activities other than special education and related services may and may not be provided with IDEA Part B funds both prior to and during a COVID-19 outbreak?

Answer: IDEA Part B funds may be used for activities that directly relate to providing, and ensuring the continuity of, special education and related services to children with disabilities. For example, an LEA may use IDEA Part B funds to disseminate health and COVID-19 information that is specifically related to children with disabilities, to develop emergency plans for children with disabilities, or to provide other information (e.g., guidance on coordination of the provision of services in alternate locations as described in Question A-5) to parties who may need such information, including school staff responsible for implementing IEPs, parents of eligible children, and staff in alternate locations where special education and related services may be provided. LEAs, however, may not use IDEA Part B funds to develop or distribute general COVID-19 guidance or to carry out activities that are not specific to children with disabilities (e.g., general COVID-19 activities for all children and staff). Additionally, LEAs may not use IDEA Part B funds to administer future COVID-19 vaccinations to any children, including children with disabilities.

B. IDEA Part C and COVID-19

Question B-1: Must a state lead agency continue to provide early intervention services to infants and toddlers with disabilities during a COVID-19 outbreak if the offices are closed?

Answer: If the offices of the state lead agency or the EIS program or provider are closed, then Part C services would not need to be provided to infants and toddlers with disabilities and their families during that period of time. If the lead agency's offices are open but the offices of the EIS program or provider in a specific geographical area are closed due to public health and safety concerns as a result of a COVID-19 outbreak in that area, the EIS program or provider would not be required to provide services during the closure. If the offices remain open, but Part C services cannot be provided in a particular location (such as in the child's home), by a particular EIS provider, or to a particular child who is infected with COVID-19, then the lead agency must ensure the continuity of services by, for example, providing services in an alternate location, by using a different EIS provider, or through alternate means, such as consultative services to the parent.

Additionally, once the offices reopen, the service coordinator and EIS providers for each child must determine if the child's service needs have changed and determine whether the individualized family service plan (IFSP) team needs to meet to review the child's IFSP to determine whether any changes are needed. If offices are closed for an extended period and services are not provided for an extended period, the IFSP team must meet under 34 CFR § 303.342(b)(1) to determine if changes are needed to the IFSP and to determine whether compensatory services are needed to address the infant or toddler's developmental delay.

Question B-2: What should a state lead agency or EIS program provider do to provide Part C services if its offices are open, but it cannot provide services in accordance with an infant's or toddler's IFSP during a COVID-19 outbreak?

Answer: If the offices remain open, but Part C services cannot be provided in a particular location (such as in the child's home), by a particular EIS provider, or to a particular child who is infected with COVID-19, then the lead agency must ensure the continuity of services, on a case-by-case basis and consistent with protecting the health and safety of the student and those providing services to the student. As an example, the lead agency may consider providing services in an alternate location, by using a different EIS provider, or through alternate means, such as consultative service to the parent. Once services are fully resumed, the service coordinator and EIS providers for each child must assess the child to determine if the child's service needs have changed and to determine whether the IFSP Team needs to meet to review the child's IFSP to identify whether changes to the IFSP are needed. If the offices are closed and services are not provided for an extended period, the IFSP Team must meet under 34 CFR § 303.342(b)(1) to determine if changes are needed to the IFSP and to determine whether compensatory services are needed.

If an EIS provider cannot provide Part C services in the child's home during a COVID-19 outbreak, but the EIS program or provider determines that it is safe to provide face-to-face Part C services in another environment such as a hospital or medical clinic, then the child could receive temporary services at the hospital or clinic. Additionally, if the lead agency or EIS provider determines that face-to-face Part C services should not be provided for a period of time, then the EIS provider or service coordinator may consult with the parent through a teleconference or other alternative method (such as e-mail or video conference), consistent with privacy interests, to provide consultative services, guidance, and advice as needed. However, determining how to provide Part C services in a manner that is consistent with the most updated public health and safety guidance is left to the discretion of the lead agency and the EIS program and provider serving a particular child and family.

Question B-3: What activities other than service provision may and may not be provided with IDEA Part C funds both prior to and during a potential COVID-19 outbreak?

Answer: IDEA Part C funds may be used for activities that directly relate to providing, and ensuring the continuity of, Part C services to eligible children and their families. The state may use IDEA Part C funds to disseminate health and COVID-19 information to relevant parties, develop emergency plans to support the provision and continuity of Part C services, or provide other information (e.g., how the lead agency staff or EIS programs or providers may provide alternate services or services in alternate locations as described in Question B-2) to relevant parties who need this information. Relevant parties may include parents of eligible children, childcare centers, staff in other locations where early intervention services are provided, EIS programs and providers, and primary referral sources. Other activities that relate to service provision, including the provision of service coordination, evaluations, and assessments, may also be funded. The state may not, however, use IDEA Part C funds to administer future COVID-19 vaccinations as it is a medical service under 34 CFR §303.13(c)(3).

2.2.2

UNITED STATES DEPARTMENT OF EDUCATION

OFFICE FOR CIVIL RIGHTS

OFFICE OF SPECIAL EDUCATION AND REHABILITATIVE SERVICES

March 21, 2020

Supplemental Fact Sheet

Addressing the Risk of COVID-19 in Preschool, Elementary and Secondary Schools While Serving Children with Disabilities

We recognize that educational institutions are straining to address the challenges of this national emergency. We also know that educators and parents are striving to provide a sense of normality while seeking ways to ensure that all students have access to meaningful educational opportunities even under these difficult circumstances. No one wants to have learning coming to a halt across America due to the COVID-19 outbreak, and the U.S. Department of Education (Department) does not want to stand in the way of good faith efforts to educate students on-line.

The Department stands ready to offer guidance, technical assistance, and information on any available flexibility, within the confines of the law, to ensure that all students, including students with disabilities, continue receiving excellent education during this difficult time. The Department's Office for Civil Rights (OCR) and the Office of Special Education and Rehabilitative Services (OSERS) have previously issued non-regulatory guidance addressing these issues.[1,2]

---

1. *See* Fact Sheet: Addressing the Risk of COVID-19 in Schools While Protecting the Civil Rights of Students (March 2020).
2. OCR Short Webinar on Online Education and Website Accessibility Webinar (Length: 00:07:08) (March 16, 2020); Questions and Answers on Providing Services to Children with Disabilities During the COVID-19 Outbreak (March 12, 2020); Fact Sheet: Impact of COVID-19 on Assessments and Accountability under the Elementary and Secondary Education Act (March 12, 2020); and Letter to Education Leaders on Preventing and Addressing Potential Discrimination Associated with COVID-19.

At the outset, OCR and OSERS must address a serious misunderstanding that has recently circulated within the educational community. As school districts nationwide take necessary steps to protect the health and safety of their students, many are moving to virtual or online education (distance instruction). Some educators, however, have been reluctant to provide any distance instruction because they believe that federal disability law presents insurmountable barriers to remote education. This is simply not true. We remind schools they should not opt to close or decline to provide distance instruction, at the expense of students, to address matters pertaining to services for students with disabilities. Rather, school systems must make local decisions that take into consideration the health, safety, and well-being of all their students and staff.

To be clear: ensuring compliance with the Individuals with Disabilities Education Act (IDEA),[3] Section 504 of the Rehabilitation Act (Section 504), and Title II of the Americans with Disabilities Act should not prevent any school from offering educational programs through distance instruction.

School districts must provide a free and appropriate public education (FAPE) consistent with the need to protect the health and safety of students with disabilities and those individuals providing education, specialized instruction, and related services to these students. In this unique and ever-changing environment, OCR and OSERS recognize that these exceptional circumstances may affect how all educational and related services and supports are provided, and the Department will offer flexibility where possible. However, school districts must remember that the provision of FAPE may include, as appropriate, special education and related services provided through distance instruction provided virtually, online, or telephonically.

The Department understands that, during this national emergency, schools may not be able to provide all services in the same manner they are typically provided. While some schools might choose to safely, and in accordance with state law, provide certain IEP services to some students in person, it may be unfeasible or unsafe for some institutions, during current emergency school closures, to provide hands-on physical therapy, occupational therapy, or tactile sign language educational services. Many disability-related modifications and services may be effectively provided online. These may include, for instance, extensions of time for assignments, videos with accurate captioning or embedded sign language interpreting, accessible reading materials, and many speech or language services through video conferencing.

It is important to emphasize that federal disability law allows for flexibility in determining how to meet the individual needs of students with disabilities. The determination of how FAPE is to be provided may need to be different in this time of unprecedented national emergency. As mentioned above, FAPE may be provided consistent with the need to protect the health and safety of students with disabilities and those individuals providing special education and related services to students. Where, due to the global pandemic and resulting closures of schools, there has been an inevitable delay in providing services—or even making decisions about how to

---

3. References to IDEA in this document include both Part B and Part C. [OCR-000116]

provide services—IEP teams (as noted in the March 12, 2020 guidance) must make an individualized determination whether and to what extent compensatory services may be needed when schools resume normal operations.

Finally, although federal law requires distance instruction to be accessible to students with disabilities, it does not mandate specific methodologies. Where technology itself imposes a barrier to access or where educational materials simply are not available in an accessible format, educators may still meet their legal obligations by providing children with disabilities equally effective alternate access to the curriculum or services provided to other students. For example, if a teacher who has a blind student in her class is working from home and cannot distribute a document accessible to that student, she can distribute to the rest of the class an inaccessible document and, if appropriate for the student, read the document over the phone to the blind student or provide the blind student with an audio recording of a reading of the document aloud.

The Department encourages parents, educators, and administrators to collaborate creatively to continue to meet the needs of students with disabilities. Consider practices such as distance instruction, teletherapy and tele-intervention, meetings held on digital platforms, online options for data tracking, and documentation. In addition, there are low-tech strategies that can provide for an exchange of curriculum-based resources, instructional packets, projects, and written assignments.

The Department understands that, during this declared national emergency, there may be additional questions about meeting the requirements of federal civil rights law; where we can offer flexibility, we will. OSERS has provided the attached list with information on those IDEA timeframes that may be extended.

OSERS' technical assistance centers are ready to address your questions regarding the IDEA and best practices and alternate models for providing special education and related services, including through distance instruction. For questions pertaining to Part C of IDEA, states should contact the Early Childhood Technical Assistance Center (ECTA) at ectacenter.org. For Part B of IDEA, states should contact the National Center for Systemic Improvement (NCSI) at ncsi.wested.org.

If you have questions for OCR, want additional information or technical assistance, or believe that a school is violating federal civil rights law, you may reach out through email at OCRWebAccessTA@ed.gov, call your regional office (https://ocrcas.ed.gov/contact-ocr), or visit the website of the Department of Education's OCR at www.ed.gov/ocr. You may contact OCR at (800) 421–3481 (TDD: 800–877–8339), at ocr@ed.gov, or contact OCR's Outreach, Prevention, Education and Non-discrimination (OPEN) Center at OPEN@ed.gov. You may also fill out a complaint form online at www.ed.gov/ocr/complaintintro.html.

Additional information specific to the COVID-19 pandemic may be found online at https://www.ed.gov/coronavirus.

IDEA Timelines

As a general principle, during this unprecedented national emergency, public agencies are encouraged to work with parents to reach mutually agreeable extensions of time, as appropriate.

Part B of IDEA

State Complaints

Absent agreement by the parties, a state may be able to extend the 60-day timeline for complaint resolution if exceptional circumstances exist with respect to a particular complaint. 34 C.F.R. § 300.152(b)(1). Although the Department has previously advised that unavailability of staff is not an exceptional circumstance that would warrant an extension of the 60-day complaint resolution timeline, the COVID-19 pandemic could be deemed an exceptional circumstance if a large number of SEA staff are unavailable or absent for an extended period of time.

Due Process Hearings

When a parent files a due process complaint, the LEA must convene a resolution meeting within 15 days of receiving notice of the parent's complaint, unless the parties agree in writing to waive the meeting or to use mediation. 34 C.F.R. § 300.510(a). While the IDEA specifically mentions circumstances in which the 30-day resolution period can be adjusted in 34 C.F.R. § 300.510(c), it does not prevent the parties from mutually agreeing to extend the timeline because of unavoidable delays caused by the COVID-19 pandemic.

Additionally, although a hearing decision must be issued and mailed to the parties 45 days after the expiration of the 30-day resolution period or an adjusted resolution period, a hearing officer may grant a specific extension of time at the request of either party to the hearing. 34 C.F.R. § 300.515(a) and (c).

Individualized Education Programs (IEPs)

If a child has been found eligible to receive services under the IDEA, the IEP Team must meet and develop an initial IEP within 30 days of a determination that the child needs special education and related services. 34 C.F.R. § 300.323(c)(1).

IEPs also must be reviewed annually. 34 C.F.R. §300.324(b)(1). However, parents and an IEP Team may agree to conduct IEP meetings through alternate means, including videoconferencing or conference telephone calls. 34 C.F.R. §300.328. Again, we encourage school teams and parents to work collaboratively and creatively to meet IEP timeline requirements.

Most importantly, in making changes to a child's IEP after the annual IEP Team meeting, because of the COVID-19 pandemic, the parent of a child with a disability and the public agency may agree to not convene an IEP Team meeting for the purposes of making those changes, and instead develop a written document to amend or modify the child's current IEP. 34 C.F.R. §300.324(a)(4)(i).

Initial Eligibility Determination

An initial evaluation must be conducted within 60 days of receiving parental consent under IDEA, or within the state established timeline within which the evaluation must be conducted. 34 C.F.R. § 300.301(c). Once the evaluation is completed, IDEA does not contain an explicit timeline for making the eligibility determination but does require that the IEP be developed in accordance with 34 C.F.R. §§ 300.320–300.324 (34 C.F.R. § 300.306(c)(2)).

Reevaluations

A reevaluation of each child with a disability must be conducted at least every three years, unless the parents and the public agency agree that a reevaluation is unnecessary. 34 C.F.R. § 300.303(b)(2). However, when appropriate, any reevaluation may be conducted through a review of existing evaluation data, and this review may occur without a meeting and without obtaining parental consent, unless it is determined that additional assessments are needed. 34 C.F.R. §300.305(a).

Part C of IDEA

State Complaints

Under 303.433(b)(1)(i), the lead agency's state Complaint procedures permit an extension of the 60-day timeline for a written decision if "exceptional circumstances exist with respect to a particular complaint" or the parent or organization and the agency or early intervention services (EIS) provider agree to extend the time for engaging in mediation.

Due Process Hearings

A state may choose to adopt Part B procedures for Due Process resolution under 34 C.F.R. §§303.440–303.449 or Part C procedures under 34 C.F.R. §§303.435–303.438. Conditions for extending the applicable timelines are similar under both sets of procedures.

Under 34 C.F.R. §303.447(c), the hearing or review officer may grant specific extensions of the Due Process timeline at the request of either party. Under 34 C.F.R. §303.447(d), each hearing and each review involving oral argument must be conducted at a time and place that is reasonably convenient to the parents and child involved.

Section 303.437 (a) and (c) provides similar language regarding scheduling a hearing at a time and place convenient to the parents and hearing officers granting extensions at the request of either party.

Initial Eligibility/Individual Family Service Plan (IFSP)

Under 34 C.F.R. §303.310, the initial evaluation and assessments of child and family, as well as the initial IFSP meeting, must be completed within 45 days of the lead agency receiving the referral. However, under 34 C.F.R. §303.310(a), the 45-day timeline does not apply if the family is unavailable due to "exceptional family circumstances that are documented" in the child's early intervention (EI) records.

The Department has previously provided guidance to states indicating that weather or natural disasters may constitute "exceptional family circumstances." The COVID-19 pandemic could be considered an "exceptional family circumstance."

2.2.3

UNITED STATES DEPARTMENT OF EDUCATION

TO: State Assessment Directors
  State Title I Directors
  State Special Education Directors

FROM: Patrick Rooney
  Director, School Support and Accountability
  Office of Elementary and Secondary Education
  Laurie VanderPloeg
  Director, Office Special Education Programs
  Office of Special Education and Rehabilitative Services

DATE: June 9, 2020

SUBJECT: Additional Information Regarding the Requirements to Request a Waiver for the 2020–21 School Year (SY) from the One Percent Cap on the Percentage of Students With the Most Significant Cognitive Disabilities Who May Be Assessed with an Alternate Assessment Aligned with Alternate Academic Achievement Standards (AA-AAAS)

We understand that State educational agencies (SEAs) are facing unprecedented challenges right now due to the impacts of the national pandemic caused by the novel Coronavirus Disease 2019, COVID-19, and that those challenges will likely continue into the coming school year. We at the U.S. Department of Education (Department) want to commend you for your efforts to ensure that learning continues for all students and we appreciate the difficulties you are facing. In this memorandum, we are providing information regarding the submission of waiver requests for the 1.0 percent cap on AAAAAS participation in the 2020–21 SY, particularly in light of the waivers that were granted this spring from the requirement to administer statewide assessments in SY 2019–20.

Section 612(a)(16)(C) of the Individuals with Disabilities Education Act (IDEA) requires that States have developed and implemented guidelines for the participation of children with disabilities in AAAAAS for those children who cannot participate in regular assessments with accommodations as indicated in their respective individualized education programs (IEPs). Title I of the Elementary and Secondary Education Act of 1965 (ESEA) requires that only students with the most significant cognitive disabilities may take an AA-AAAS; it also limits the number of students that a State may assess with an AA-AAAS to no more than 1.0 percent of all students in the grades assessed in a State.[4] This requirement was first in effect for SY 2017–18. The Department recognizes, however, that most States were exceeding this percentage prior to SY 2017–18 and that it would likely take several years for a State to come into compliance with this requirement. As a result, the ESEA permits the Department to grant a waiver to a State, if it meets certain statutory and regulatory requirements, to assess more than 1.0 percent of students on an AA-AAAS.

In May 2017, the Department provided information regarding the procedures for a State to apply for such a waiver.[5] In August 2018, the Department published additional information for States that may wish to apply to extend their existing one-year waiver for an additional year.[6] This memorandum clarified the requirements for such an extension, which include demonstrating substantial progress towards achieving each component of the prior year's plan and timeline, to ensure that the State is making progress towards meeting the 1.0 percent cap and assessing only students with the most significant cognitive disabilities with an AA-AAAS. The Department has posted all waiver requests and the Department's response for SYs 2017–18, 2018–19, and 2019–20 at https://oese.ed.gov/offices/office-of-formula-grants/school-support-and-accountability/essa-state-plansassessment-waivers/.

In March 2020, COVID-19 resulted in widespread and extended school closures. As a result, it was not feasible for most schools to administer annual statewide assessments. The Department invited States to request a waiver for SY 2019–20 of the assessment requirements in ESEA section 1111(b)(2) of the ESEA, the accountability and school identification requirements in ESEA sections 1111(c)(4) and 1111(d)(2)(C)-(D), and related reporting requirements in ESEA section 1111(h). Every State applied for and received this waiver.

States Applying for a New Waiver

The requirements and procedures to request a waiver from the 1.0 percent cap are unchanged and are provided in detail in the prior documents from May 2017 and August 2018. States applying for a new waiver should ensure that their request addresses each requirement detailed in those documents, including the requirements in section 8401 of the ESEA related to public comment.

The waiver request must include data from the current or previous school year[7] to show the number and percentage of students overall and from each subgroup of students who will take or took the AAAAAS with respect to each subject for which the State seeks a waiver. However, we understand that most States will not have data for SY 2019–20, so they will not be able to provide AA-AAAS data from the previous school year.

---

4. See http://www2.ed.gov/documents/essa-act-of-1965.pdf.
5. See https://www2.ed.gov/admins/lead/account/saa/onepercentcapmemo51617.pdf.
6. See https://oese.ed.gov/files/2020/02/ossstateassessmentltr.pdf.
7. For example, a State could have applied for a waiver for SY 2018–19 school year using data from either 2018–19 (current school year) or 2017–18 (previous school year).

For that reason, the Department encourages a State to use current year (2020–21) IEP[8] or test registration data to make a credible estimate of the number and percentage of students (including by subgroup, if possible) who will take the AA-AAAS in SY 2020–21 or who would have taken the AAAAAS in SY 2019–20 if testing had been conducted. States should also provide actual participation data on this population, overall and by subgroup, from SY 2018–19. An example of such data is provided in appendix A of this memorandum. The Department believes that using IEP/test registration data to create a credible estimate for SY 2019–20 or 2020–21 participation rates may help the State demonstrate that they are making progress in reducing the percentage of AA-AAAS participation.

As in previous years, the State will also need to provide data to show that the State has assessed the achievement of at least 95 percent of **all students** and 95 percent of **children with disabilities** who are enrolled in grades for which the assessment is required. This percentage must include all students assessed with the general assessment and the AA-AAAS for each requested subject. Because States will not have valid participation data for SY 2019–20, the State will need to rely on participation data from SY 2018–19.

The State will need to provide evidence that the SEA has verified that **each LEA** that the State anticipates will assess more than 1.0 percent of its assessed students in any subject using an AA-AAAS followed the State's guidelines for participation in the AA-AAAS[9] and will address any disproportionality in the percentage of students in any subgroup taking an AA-AAAS. This can be done in SY 2020–21 and must have occurred before submission of the waiver request.

Finally, the State will need to provide a plan and timeline with clear, actionable steps and milestones that includes:

- A clear description of how the State will improve the implementation of its guidelines for participation in the AA-AAAS, including by reviewing and, if necessary, revising its definition of students with the most significant cognitive disabilities (see 34 CFR 200.6(d)(1)), so that the State meets the 1.0 percent cap in each subject for which assessments are administered in future school years;
- A clear description of how it will monitor and regularly evaluate each LEA to ensure that the LEA provides sufficient training such that school staff who participate as members of an IEP team or other placement team understand and implement the guidelines established by the State for participation in an AA-AAAS so that all students are appropriately assessed; and
- A clear description of how the State will address any disproportionality in the percentage of students taking an AA-AAAS as identified through the data provided.

---

8. In accordance with IDEA, the IEP team determines whether a child shall take an alternate assessment on a particular State or districtwide assessment of student achievement, and the IEP team must document such a decision in the child's IEP.
9. 34 CFR 200.6(d), consistent with section 612(a)(16)(C) of the Individuals with Disabilities Education Act (IDEA).

States Applying to Extend a Waiver Granted or Extended in a Prior Year

A State that wishes to request an extension of a waiver that it received in a prior year should provide updated information regarding each requirement in the previous year's submission. In preparing a waiver renewal request, the State must continue to meet each requirement associated with the first waiver it received from this requirement. Additionally, a State must demonstrate substantial progress towards achieving each component of the prior year's plan and timeline. **If a State's plan and timeline was disrupted due to COVID-19, its waiver request should explain the impact of those disruptions.**

As noted above, the Department encourages the State to use current year IEP or test registration data to make a credible estimate of the number and percentage of students (including by subgroup, if possible) who will take the AA-AAAS in SY 2020–21 or who would have taken the AA-AAAS in SY 2019–20 if testing had been conducted. States should also provide actual participation data, overall and by subgroup, from SY 2018–19.

States Denied a Waiver in SY 2019–20

States that were **denied** a 1.0 percent cap waiver in SY 2019–20 will need to follow the instructions for applying for a new waiver if they wish to seek a waiver in SY 2020–21. States should be sure to address the concern that led to the denial of their SY 2019–20 waiver request.

States Seeking a Combination New Waiver and an Extension of a Waiver

Some States were denied or did not apply for a waiver in a particular subject area (typically due to participation rates below 95 percent) but received a waiver in other subject areas. As in previous years, this will be treated as a combination new/extension waiver request and all of the applicable requirements apply to each subject area included in the State's request. That is, for the waivers the State requested be extended, the State must provide information described in "States Applying to Extend a Waiver Granted or Extended in a Prior Year." For the subjects that are new waivers, the State must provide information described in "States Applying for a New Waiver."

States with Early Testing Windows

The Department reminds States that a request for a waiver of the 1.0 percent cap requirement, whether new or extension, must be submitted 90 days before the beginning of the State's testing window. For a State that tests throughout the year, this deadline *may* occur during summer 2020. The State should follow this requirement even if all of the necessary information is not yet available. The Department encourages the State to explain in its requests any missing information and provide a clear timeline for when the data will become available. Once the Department receives the required information, the waiver will be considered for approval.

States with questions about these waiver requests should contact the Office of School Support and Accountability's Assessment Team at ESEA.Assessment@ed.gov. All requests for 1.0 percent cap waivers should be submitted to ESEA.Assessment@ed.gov. Thank you for your continued commitment to our nation's students.

Appendix A

TABLE 2.1 Example of Data Display to Support a State's Waiver Request to Exceed the 1.0 Percent Cap on AAAAAS Participation.

Group	Total Grades 3–8 and 10 R/LA 2018–19	Total Children w Disabilities Grades 3–8 and 10 R/LA 2018–19	# Take State R/LA AA-AAAS Gr. 3–8 and 10 2018–19	% Taking State R/LA AA-AAAS Gr. 3–8 and 10 2018–19
All students	475,611	78,924	7,453	1.57% (= 7,453/475,611)
English learners	41,232	9,812	911	2.21%
Black	46,258	9,933	1,116	2.41%
Hispanic	95,464	22,163	2,168	2.27%
Asian	31,956	2,817	432	1.35%
White	260,701	57,246	3,919	1.50%
Econ. Disadv.	172,190	44,725	4,754	2.76%

Group	Estimated* Total Grades 3–8 and 10 R/LA 2019–20	Estimated* Total Children w Disabilities Grades 3–8 and 10 R/LA 2019–20	Estimated* # Taking State R/LA AA-AAAS Gr. 3–8 and 10 2019–20	Estimated* % Taking State R/LA AA-AAAS Gr. 3–8 and 10 2019–20
All students	476,834	79,412	7,021	1.47% (= 7,021/476,834)
English learners	42,491	10,011	798	1.88%
Black	45,876	10,438	986	2.15%
Hispanic	96,348	23,045	2,053	2.13%
Asian	31,123	2,790	401	1.29%
White	263,128	58,291	3,919	1.49%
Econ. Disadv.	178,897	45,865	4,234	2.37%

* Estimates are based on test registration; depending on the availability of State data, this could be 2019–20 or 2020–21 test registration data.
(*Note*: This is sample data only, it does not represent any single State's data)

2.2.4

UNITED STATES DEPARTMENT OF EDUCATION

OFFICE OF SPECIAL EDUCATION AND REHABILITATIVE SERVICES
OFFICE OF SPECIAL EDUCATION PROGRAMS

June 30, 2020

The Office of Special Education Programs (OSEP), within the U.S. Department of Education's (Department) Office of Special Education and Rehabilitative Services, issues this Question and Answer (Q & A) document in response to inquiries concerning implementation of the Individuals with Disabilities Education Act (IDEA) Part B dispute resolution procedures in the current COVID-19 environment.

This Q & A document does not impose any additional requirements beyond those included in applicable law and regulations. It does not create or confer any rights for or on any person. The responses presented in this document generally constitute informal guidance representing the interpretation of the Department of the applicable statutory or regulatory requirements in the context of the specific facts presented here and are not legally binding and does not establish a policy or rule that would apply in all circumstances.

To review other Q & A documents that OSEP has provided related to COVID-19, please visit https://sites.ed.gov/idea/topic-areas/#COVID-19. Additional information specific to the COVID-19 pandemic may be found online at https://www.ed.gov/coronavirus.

IDEA PART B DISPUTE RESOLUTION PROCEDURES

Q1. How can parents and public agencies resolve disagreements regarding special education matters while school buildings and other public facilities are closed due to the pandemic?

OSEP encourages parents and local educational agencies (LEAs) to work collaboratively, in the best interest of children with disabilities, to resolve disagreements that may occur when working to provide a positive educational experience for all children, including children with disabilities.

In its March 21, 2020 Supplemental Fact Sheet, the Department recognized that during this national emergency, schools may not be able to provide all services in the same manner that they are typically provided, and encouraged parents, educators, and administrators to collaborate creatively to continue to meet the needs of children with disabilities. Timely communication between parents and public agency staff can often help resolve disagreements that may arise regarding the educational services provided to a child with a disability during the pandemic. However, when those informal efforts prove unsuccessful, IDEA's three dispute resolution mechanisms—mediation, State complaint, and due process complaint procedures—are available.

Q2. Is a State educational agency (SEA) permitted to extend the 60-day time limit for resolving a State complaint[10] due to circumstances related to the pandemic?

Yes, but only on a case-by-case basis. Under 34 C.F.R. § 300.152, a State's minimum State complaint procedures under Part B of IDEA must include a 60-day timeline for complaint resolution. The regulations specify two allowable reasons for extending the 60-day time limit: (1) if exceptional circumstances exist with respect to a particular complaint; or (2) if the parent (or individual or organization, if mediation or other alternative means of dispute resolution are available to the individual or organization under State procedures) and the public agency involved agree to extend the time to engage in mediation or other alternative means of dispute resolution, if available in the State. 34 C.F.R. § 300.152(b)(1).

With regard to the "exceptional circumstances" exception to the 60-day timeline, States will need to determine on a case-by-case basis whether it is appropriate to extend the 60-day time limit for a particular complaint due to exceptional circumstances related to the pandemic or related health and safety restrictions. An SEA may not categorically determine that it will not undertake complaint resolutions during the pandemic based solely on its assumption that COVID-19 is an exceptional circumstance that would warrant an extension of the 60-day complaint resolution timeline for all complaints.

Although the Department has previously concluded that unavailability of SEA staff generally is not an exceptional circumstance that would warrant an extension of the 60-day complaint resolution timeline, conditions related to the pandemic could be deemed an exceptional circumstance with respect to a particular complaint if, for example, a large number of SEA staff are unavailable or absent for an extended period of time as a result of the pandemic, or where the SEA cannot access specific information from school/agency staff or the child's education records needed to resolve the complaint due to conditions related to the pandemic.

---

10. The requirements for State complaints are in 34 C.F.R. §§ 300.151 through 300.153.

Q3. How can parents and public agencies use IDEA's mediation procedures[11] to resolve disputes when schools and other public facilities are closed or have restrictions that prevent face-to-face meetings?

IDEA does not contain a specific timeframe in which mediation must occur so long as it is not used to deny or delay a parent's right to a hearing on the due process complaint or any other rights afforded under Part B. Because mediation is voluntary, the parties have the flexibility to identify a mutually agreeable time to meet. 34 C.F.R. § 300.506(a).

Where circumstances related to the pandemic prevent the parent or public agency representative from attending mediation in person, there is nothing in IDEA that would prevent the parties from agreeing to conduct the mediation through alternative means, such as video conferences or conference calls, if the State's procedures do not prohibit mediation from occurring in this manner.

Q4. Can the parent and LEA agree to extend the timelines applicable to the resolution process[12] given the challenges associated with school and other public facility operations during the COVID-19 pandemic?

Yes. There is nothing in IDEA that would prevent the parent and public agency from mutually agreeing to extend the 15-day timeline for the LEA to convene a resolution meeting and the 30-day resolution period timeline when a parent files a due process complaint. If the parties are unable to meet in person or through virtual means (discussed in Q5), they could mutually agree to extend the 15-day timeline for the resolution meeting and the 30-day resolution period until a face-to-face meeting could occur.

However, IDEA does not permit an extension of the 7-day resolution meeting timeline or the 15-day resolution period for expedited due process complaints that address disputes about disciplinary removals of students with disabilities.

Q5. Can the parent and LEA agree to hold a resolution meeting virtually, rather than face-to-face?

Yes. Where the circumstances related to the pandemic prevent the parent or public agency representative from attending the resolution meeting in person, it would be appropriate for the public agency to offer to use alternative means, such as video conferences or conference calls, subject to the parent's agreement, consistent with 34 C.F.R. § 300.328. Resolution meetings related to expedited due process complaints involving discipline may also be conducted through video conferences or conference calls, subject to the parent's agreement.

---

11. The requirements for mediation are in 34 C.F.R. § 300.506.
12. For due process complaints, the requirements for the LEA to convene a resolution meeting within 15 days and the 30-day resolution period are in 34 C.F.R. § 300.510. The requirements for convening resolution meetings within 7 days and the 15-day resolution period for expedited due process complaints are in 34 C.F.R. § 300.532.

Q6. May due process hearings[13] be conducted virtually when schools and other public facilities are closed or have restrictions that prevent face-to-face meetings?

Yes. A State could permit hearings on due process complaints to be conducted through video conferences or conference calls, if a hearing officer concludes that such procedures are consistent with legal practice in the State. 34 C.F.R. § 300.511(c)(1)(iii). A hearing conducted virtually must ensure a parent's right to an impartial due process hearing consistent with all requirements in 34 C.F.R. §§ 300.511 through 300.515. If applicable, a State-level review can be conducted virtually if consistent with State procedures.

Q7. Do hearing officers, or where applicable, reviewing officers, have the authority to extend the applicable timelines for issuing decisions on due process complaints during the pandemic?

Yes. IDEA permits a hearing officer or a reviewing officer to grant specific extensions of timelines at the request of either party to the hearing or review. 34 C.F.R. § 300.515(c); see 34 C.F.R. § 300.515(a)-(b) for applicable timelines. There is no IDEA requirement that both parties agree to the extension request, but the hearing officer or reviewing officer must document the length of the extension and the reason it was provided.

While a hearing or State-level review of an expedited due process complaint may be conducted through video conferences or conference calls if consistent with legal practice in the State, IDEA makes no similar provision for extending relevant timelines for hearings or reviews in the context of expedited due process complaints.

---

13. The requirements for hearings on due process complaints are in 34 C.F.R. §§ 300.507 through 300.516. The requirements for hearings on expedited due process complaints are in 34 C.F.R. §§ 300.532 through 300.533.

2.2.5

UNITED STATES DEPARTMENT OF EDUCATION
OFFICE OF SPECIAL EDUCATION AND REHABILITATIVE SERVICES
OFFICE OF SPECIAL EDUCATION PROGRAMS

June 22, 2020

The Office of Special Education Programs (OSEP), within the U.S. Department of Education's (Department) Office of Special Education and Rehabilitative Services, issues this Question and Answer (Q & A) document in response to inquiries concerning implementation of the Individuals with Disabilities Education Act (IDEA) Part C dispute resolution procedures in the current COVID-19 environment.

This Q & A document does not impose any additional requirements beyond those included in applicable law and regulations. It does not create or confer any rights for or on any person. The responses presented in this document generally constitute informal guidance representing the interpretation of the Department of the applicable statutory or regulatory requirements in the context of the specific facts presented here and are not legally binding and does not establish a policy or rule that would apply in all circumstances.

To review other Q & A documents that OSEP has provided related to COVID-19, please visit https://sites.ed.gov/idea/topic-areas/#COVID-19. Additional information specific to the COVID-19 pandemic may be found online at https://www.ed.gov/coronavirus.

IDEA PART C DISPUTE RESOLUTION PROCEDURES

Q1. How can parents, State lead agencies (State LAs), and early intervention service (EIS) providers resolve disagreements regarding IDEA Part C early intervention matters due to conditions related to the public health response to the pandemic?

OSEP encourages parents, State LAs, and EIS providers to work collaboratively, in the best interest of infants and toddlers with disabilities, to resolve disagreements that may occur when working to provide positive early intervention experiences. In its March 2020 Questions and Answers on Providing Services to Children with Disabilities During the Coronavirus Disease 2019 Outbreak, the Department addressed the provision of early intervention services during the pandemic. We recognize that, during this national emergency, State LAs and EIS providers may not be able to provide all services in the same manner they are typically provided, and encourage parents, service providers, and administrators to collaborate creatively to continue to the meet the needs of infants and toddlers with disabilities and their families. Timely communication between parents, State LA staff, and EIS providers can often help resolve disagreements that may arise regarding the early intervention services provided during the pandemic. However, when those informal efforts prove unsuccessful, IDEA's three dispute resolution mechanisms—mediation, State complaint, and due process complaint procedures—are available.

Q2. Is a State LA permitted to extend the 60-day time limit for resolving State complaints[14] due to circumstances related to the pandemic?

Yes, but only on a case-by-case basis. Under 34 C.F.R. § 303.433(a), a State's minimum State complaint procedures under Part C of IDEA must include a 60-day timeline for complaint resolution. The regulations specify two allowable reasons for extending the 60-day time limit: (1) if exceptional circumstances exist with respect to a particular complaint; or (2) if the parent (or individual or organization, if mediation is available to the individual or organization under State procedures) and the State LA, public agency, or EIS provider agree to extend the time to engage in mediation pursuant to 34 C.F.R. § 303.433(b)(1).

With regard to the "exceptional circumstances" exception to the 60-day timeline, States will need to determine on a case-by-case basis whether it is appropriate to extend the 60-day time limit for a particular complaint due to exceptional circumstances related to the pandemic or related health and safety restrictions. A State LA may not categorically determine that it will not undertake complaint resolutions during the pandemic based solely on its assumption that COVID-19 is an exceptional circumstance that would warrant an extension of the 60-day complaint resolution timeline for all complaints.

A State LA may extend the 60-day time limit due to exceptional circumstances such as a governmentwide shutdown, if the State LA needs additional information under 34 C.F.R. § 303.433(a)(2) and the relevant party(ies) is (are) unavailable due to hospitalization, or a parent complainant is unavailable due to illness or other documented reason and cannot provide the additional information under 34 C.F.R. § 303.433(a)(2). See 76 Fed. Reg. 61410, 60215 (Sept. 28, 2011). Although the Department has previously concluded that unavailability of State LA staff generally is not an exceptional circumstance that would warrant an extension of the 60-day complaint resolution timeline, conditions related to the pandemic could be deemed an exceptional circumstance with respect to a particular complaint if, for example, a large number of State LA staff are unavailable or absent for an extended period of time as a result of the pandemic, or where the State LA cannot access specific information from EIS providers

---

14. The requirements for State complaints are in 34 C.F.R. §§ 303.432 through 303.434.

or the child's early intervention records needed to resolve the complaint due to conditions related to the pandemic.

Q3. How can parents, the State LA, and EIS providers use IDEA's mediation[15] procedures to resolve disputes when agencies and other public facilities are closed or have restrictions that prevent face-to-face meetings?

IDEA does not contain a specific timeframe in which mediation must occur so long as it is not used to deny or delay a parent's right to a due process hearing or to deny any other rights afforded under Part C. Because mediation is voluntary, the parties have the flexibility to identify a mutually agreeable time to meet. 34 C.F.R. § 303.431(b)(1). Where the circumstances related to the pandemic prevent the parent, State LA representative, or EIS provider from attending mediation in person, there is nothing in IDEA that would prevent the parties from agreeing to conduct the mediation through alternative means, such as video conferences or conference calls, if the State's procedures do not prohibit mediation from occurring in this manner.

Due Process Hearings[16]: When the Lead Agency Has Adopted Part C Due Process Procedures

Q4. May due process hearings be conducted virtually when agencies and other public facilities are closed or have restrictions that prevent face-to-face meetings?

Yes. A State LA could permit hearings on due process complaints to be conducted through video conferences or conference calls, if a hearing officer concludes that such procedures are consistent with legal practice in the State. A hearing conducted virtually must ensure a parent's right to an impartial due process hearing consistent with all requirements in 34 C.F.R. §§ 303.435 through 300.437.

Q5. Do hearing officers have the authority to extend the 30-day timeline for issuing decisions on due process complaints during the pandemic?

Yes. IDEA permits a hearing officer to grant specific extensions of the 30-day timeline at the request of either party to the hearing. 34 C.F.R. § 303.437(c). There is no IDEA requirement that both parties agree to the extension request, but the hearing officer must document the length of the extension and the reason it was provided.

---

15. The requirements for mediation are in 34 C.F.R. § 303.431.
16. The requirements for States that choose to adopt the Part C due process hearing procedures are in 34 C.F.R. §§ 303.435 through 303.438.

Resolution Process[17] and Due Process Hearings[18]: When the Lead Agency Has Adopted Part B Due Process Procedures

Q6. Can the parent and EIS provider agree to extend the timelines applicable to the resolution process given the challenges associated with agency and other public facility operations during the COVID-19 pandemic?

Yes. There is nothing in IDEA that would prevent the parent and EIS provider from mutually agreeing to extend the 15-day timeline for the State LA or EIS provider to convene a resolution meeting and the 30-day resolution period timeline when a parent files a due process complaint. If the parties are unable to meet in person or through virtual means (discussed in Q7), they could mutually agree to extend the 15-day timeline for the resolution meeting and the 30-day resolution period until a face-to-face meeting could occur.

Q7. Can the parent and EIS provider agree to hold a resolution meeting virtually, rather than face-to-face?

Yes. Where the circumstances related to the pandemic prevent the parent or EIS provider from attending the resolution meeting in person, it would be appropriate for the State LA to offer to use alternative means, such as video conferences or conference calls, with its use subject to the parent's agreement.

Q8. May due process hearings be conducted virtually when agencies and other public facilities are closed or have restrictions that prevent face-to-face meetings?

Yes. A State could permit hearings on due process complaints to be conducted through video conferences or conference calls, if a hearing officer concludes that such procedures are consistent with legal practice in the State. 34 C.F.R. § 303.443(c)(1)(iii). A hearing conducted virtually must ensure a parent's right to an impartial due process hearing consistent with all requirements in 34 C.F.R. §§ 303.443 through 303.448.

Q9. Do hearing officers, or where applicable, reviewing officers, have the authority to extend the applicable timelines for issuing decisions on due process complaints during the pandemic?

Yes. IDEA permits a hearing officer or a reviewing officer to grant specific extensions of timelines at the request of either party to the hearing or review. 34 C.F.R. § 303.447(c); see 34 C.F.R. § 303.447(a)–(b) for applicable timelines. There is no IDEA requirement that both parties agree to the extension request, but the hearing officer or reviewing officer must document the length of the extension and the reason it was provided.

---

17. The requirements for the resolution process applicable to States that choose to adopt the Part B due process hearing procedures are in 34 C.F.R. § 303.442.
18. The requirements for States that choose to adopt the Part B due process hearing procedures are in 34 C.F.R. §§ 303.440 through 303.448.

2.2.6

UNITED STATES DEPARTMENT OF EDUCATION

OFFICE OF SPECIAL EDUCATION AND REHABILITATIVE SERVICES
OFFICE OF SPECIAL EDUCATION PROGRAMS

June 25, 2020

The Office of Special Education Programs (OSEP), within the U.S. Department of Education's (Department) Office of Special Education and Rehabilitative Services (OSERS), issues this Question and Answer (Q & A) document in response to inquiries concerning implementation of the Individuals with Disabilities Education Act (IDEA) Part B use of funds in the current COVID-19 environment.

This Q & A document does not impose any additional requirements beyond those included in applicable law and regulations. It does not create or confer any rights for or on any person. The responses presented in this document generally constitute informal guidance representing the interpretation of the Department of the applicable statutory or regulatory requirements in the context of the specific facts presented here and are not legally binding and does not establish a policy or rule that would apply in all circumstances.

To review other Q & A documents that OSEP has provided related to COVID-19, please visit https://sites.ed.gov/idea/topic-areas/#COVID-19. Additional information specific to the COVID-19 pandemic may be found online at https://www.ed.gov/coronavirus.

IDEA PART B USE OF FUNDS

Q1. How can local educational agencies (LEAs) utilize IDEA Part B subgrant funds to address conditions caused by the COVID-19 pandemic?

IDEA Part B funds may be used only to pay the excess costs of activities that directly relate to providing, and ensuring the continuity of, special education and related services to children with disabilities.[19] For example, an LEA may use IDEA Part B funds to disseminate health and COVID-19 information that is specifically related to children with disabilities, to develop emergency plans for children with disabilities, or to provide other information (e.g., guidance on coordination of the provision of services in alternate locations[20]) to parties who may need such information.[21] LEAs may also use IDEA Part B funds to engage in activities necessary to resume the provision of special education and related services to children with disabilities. Under 34 C.F.R. § 300.202(a)(1), IDEA Part B funds provided to LEAs must be expended in accordance with IDEA. LEAs must also meet the Office of Management and Budget (OMB) Uniform Administrative Requirements, Cost Principles, and Audit Requirements for Federal Awards' (Uniform Guidance) requirements for procurement in C.F.R. §§ 200.318 through 200.326, and maintain appropriate records and cost documentation as required by 2 C.F.R. § 200.302 (financial management), 2 C.F.R. § 200.333 (retention requirements for records), and 2 C.F.R. § 200.430(i) (standards for documenting personnel expenses). Further, costs incurred that are associated with COVID-19 related reasons will be allowable only if they are reasonable, necessary, and allocable to the grant, consistent with the Federal cost principles described in the OMB Uniform Guidance (2 C.F.R. §§ 200.403, 200.404, and 200.405), adequately documented (2 C.F.R. § 200.403(g)), and do not conflict with the applicable statute and regulations.

Q2. What options are available to State educational agencies (SEAs) in using IDEA Part B funds to address additional challenges during the COVID-19 pandemic?

States have considerable flexibility in the use of IDEA Part B funds that they may set aside for "other State-level activities" under 34 C.F.R. § 300.704(b)(4)[22] that they may find beneficial during the current COVID-19 crisis. These include: (1) support for the use of technology to maximize accessibility to the general education curriculum for children with disabilities, including technology with universal design principles such as software compatible with screen readers, online tools that make electronic books accessible to individuals with disabilities, and assistive technology devices such as dedicated communication devices

---

19. For guidance on the use of Federal funds to pay for the compensation of employees and for conference, training and travel-related expenses, see https://www2.ed.gov/documents/coronavirus/factsheet-fiscal-questions.pdf.
20. See Question and Answer A-5 of the Department's Questions and Answers on Providing Services to Children with Disabilities During the COVID-19 Outbreak (March 12, 2020).
21. Parties who may need such information include school staff responsible for implementing individualized education programs (IEPs), parents of eligible children, and staff in alternate locations where special education and related services (e.g., occupational therapy, physical therapy, or speech-language pathology services) may be provided.
22. States may use a portion of the IDEA section 611 funds they reserve under 34 C.F.R. § 300.704(b)(1) for other State-level activities to carry out any of the authorized activities enumerated in 34 C.F.R. § 300.704(b)(4).

for non-verbal students with disabilities; and (2) capacity building activities directed at improving the delivery of services by LEAs to improve results for children with disabilities (34 C.F.R. § 300.704(b)(4)(iv) and (viii)).

Under these authorized activities, SEAs may elect to build the capacity of LEAs to ensure that students with disabilities have equal access to the same opportunities available to their nondisabled peers, including remote learning.

IDEA Part B funds may also be used to provide special education and related services, as well as supplementary aids and services (such as training or assistive technology), provided in the regular or remote learning setting to a child with a disability in accordance with the child's IEP, even if one or more nondisabled students benefit from those services.[23]

When expending IDEA Part B funds to procure property (such as equipment and other assets, including technological devices) and services (including potentially training on the use of remote learning platforms, or best practices for remote learning), SEAs must follow the same policies and procedures they use for procurements from their non-Federal funds, consistent with 2 C.F.R. § 200.317. SEAs must use, manage, and dispose of equipment in accordance with State laws and procedures, consistent with 2 C.F.R. § 200.313(b). See also Q3 below. In addition, SEAs must maintain appropriate records and cost documentation as required by 2 C.F.R. § 200.302 (financial management), 2 C.F.R. § 200.333 (retention requirements for records), and 2 C.F.R. § 200.430(i) (standards for documenting personnel expenses). Further, costs incurred that are associated with COVID-19 related reasons will be allowable only if they are reasonable, necessary, and allocable to the grant, consistent with the Federal cost principles described in the OMB Uniform Guidance (2 C.F.R. §§ 200.403, 200.404, and 200.405) and adequately documented (2 C.F.R. § 200.403(g)), and do not conflict with the applicable statute and regulations.

Q3. Are SEAs and LEAs able to use IDEA Part B funds to purchase equipment necessary to increase their capacity to support remote learning for students with disabilities?

OSEP acknowledges that, particularly during the COVID-19 pandemic, SEAs and their LEAs may need to purchase equipment and other assets (such as software, mobile hot spots, or devices like laptops and tablets[24]), including related assistive technology, in order to support increased accessibility to remote learning platforms for students with disabilities. Under 34 C.F.R. § 300.718(a), if OSEP determines that an IDEA Part B program will be improved by permitting

---

23. See IDEA's permissive use of funds provision in 34 C.F.R. § 300.208(a)(1). It is permissible to use IDEA Part B funds in such cases where an "incidental benefit" is provided to nondisabled children as a result of special education and related services provided under IDEA to children with disabilities. See OSEP's Aug. 5, 2013, letter to Ms. Bowman.
24. IDEA Part B funds may not be used to purchase equipment that is being provided to all students, such as laptops distributed to the entire student population of a school to facilitate remote learning. However, to the extent that students with disabilities require additional equipment, in addition to what is being provided to all students, in order to access remote learning, IDEA funds may be used to purchase the equipment to enable that access.

program funds to be used to acquire appropriate equipment,[25] (such as a dedicated communication device for an individual student with a disability), OSEP is authorized to allow the use of those funds for those purposes. Equipment and other assets purchased with IDEA Part B funds may be transferred from school to home, as needed for use by students with disabilities in remote learning settings.

If equipment expenditures fall within the scope of the prior approval already provided under OSERS' October 29, 2019, Frequently Asked Questions (FAQs) on "Prior Approval—OSEP and RSA Formula Grants,"[26] SEAs are not required to submit prior approval requests for the equipment. Under that prior approval, grantees do not need to submit prior approval requests to OSEP for equipment (defined generally as $5,000 or more per item of equipment) that is to be charged to IDEA funds and which is identified on, or directly related to the implementation of, IEPs for children and youth with disabilities, including services such as assistive technology devices listed on the IEP as well as equipment needed to provide services in accordance with the IEP. However, if an SEA must purchase equipment that goes beyond the scope of the prior approval provided in the FAQs, then the SEA must submit a detailed prior approval request to OSEP. OSEP has streamlined its current approval process to respond to the anticipated increase in requests. Similarly, under their subrecipient monitoring authority,[27] SEAs may anticipate additional prior approval requests from their LEAs regarding the use of IDEA Part B funds for the purchase of equipment, and SEAs may wish to expedite their usual procedures and practices consistent with any flexibilities afforded by the State during times of emergency.

Under 34 C.F.R. § 300.202(a)(1), IDEA Part B funds provided to LEAs must be expended in accordance with IDEA. Further, when expending IDEA Part B funds to procure property (including equipment and other assets, such as technological devices) and services (including training on the use of remote learning platforms, or best practices for remote learning), SEAs must follow the same policies and procedures they use for procurements from their non-Federal funds, consistent with 2 C.F.R. § 200.317. SEAs must use, manage, and dispose of equipment in accordance with State laws and procedures, consistent with 2 C.F.R. § 200.313(b). LEAs must meet the OMB Uniform Guidance requirements for procurement in 2 C.F.R. §§ 200.318 through 200.326, and for equipment in 2 C.F.R. §§ 200.313(c)–(e) and 200.439. Both SEAs and LEAs must also maintain appropriate records and cost documentation as required by 2 C.F.R. § 200.302 (financial management), 2 C.F.R. § 200.333 (retention requirements

---

25. Equipment is defined in the IDEA regulations at 34 C.F.R. § 300.14. Equipment is further defined in the OMB Uniform Guidance at 2 C.F.R. § 200.33.
26. Available at https://www2.ed.gov/policy/speced/guid/faq-prior-approval-10-29-2019.pdf.
27. Under the OMB Uniform Guidance requirements in 2 C.F.R. § 200.439(b)(1)–(3), SEAs have the authority, as the pass-through entity, to review and approve LEAs' requests to use IDEA Part B funds for the purchase of equipment, using the same criteria described in FAQ 12 of OSERS' October 29, 2019, FAQs on "Prior Approval –OSEP and RSA Formula Grants."

for records), and 2 C.F.R. § 200.430(i) (standards for documenting personnel expenses). Further, costs incurred that are associated with COVID-19 related reasons will be allowable only if they are reasonable, necessary, and allocable to the grant, consistent with the Federal cost principles described in the OMB Uniform Guidance (2 C.F.R. §§ 200.403, 200.404, and 200.405) and adequately documented (2 C.F.R. § 200.403(g)), and do not conflict with the applicable statute and regulations.

2.2.7

UNITED STATES DEPARTMENT OF EDUCATION
OFFICE OF SPECIAL EDUCATION AND REHABILITATIVE SERVICES
OFFICE OF SPECIAL EDUCATION PROGRAMS

June 25, 2020

The Office of Special Education Programs (OSEP), within the U.S. Department of Education's (Department) Office of Special Education and Rehabilitative Services (OSERS), issues this Question and Answer (Q & A) document in response to inquiries concerning implementation of the Individuals with Disabilities Education Act (IDEA) Part C use of funds in the current COVID-19 environment.

This Q & A document does not impose any additional requirements beyond those included in applicable law and regulations. It does not create or confer any rights for or on any person. The responses presented in this document generally constitute informal guidance representing the interpretation of the Department of the applicable statutory or regulatory requirements in the context of the specific facts presented here and are not legally binding and does not establish a policy or rule that would apply in all circumstances.

To review other Q & A documents that OSEP has provided related to COVID-19, please visit https://sites.ed.gov/idea/topic-areas/#COVID-19. Additional information specific to the COVID-19 pandemic may be found online at https://www.ed.gov/coronavirus.

IDEA PART C USE OF FUNDS

Q1. What activities can be funded using IDEA Part C to address conditions caused by the COVID-19 pandemic?

Under 34 C.F.R. § 303.501, the State lead agency (State LA) and early intervention service (EIS) provider may use IDEA Part C funds for activities or expenses that are reasonable and necessary to implement the State's early intervention program for infants and toddlers with disabilities including—

   a. For direct early intervention services for infants and toddlers with disabilities and their families under this part that are not otherwise funded through other public or private sources (subject to 34 C.F.R. §§303.510 through 303.521);
   b. To expand and improve services for infants and toddlers with disabilities and their families under this part that are otherwise available.

Additionally, IDEA Part C funds may be used for activities that directly relate to providing, and ensuring the continuity of, Part C services to eligible children and their families as well as activities that support the Statewide early intervention program including child find, public awareness, referral and evaluation, conducting child and family assessments through alternative ways, developing and disseminating information on alternative communications and service delivery options, use of videoconferencing specific to communicating and delivering, early intervention services. The State LA and EIS program and provider may also use IDEA Part C funds to disseminate health and COVID-19 information to, and respond to information requests from relevant parties, develop emergency plans to support the provision and continuity of Part C services, or provide other information (e.g., how the State LA staff or EIS programs or providers may provide services in different formats or locations as described in Question B-2 of the document titled Questions and Answers on Providing Services to Children with Disabilities During the COVID-19 Outbreak (March 12, 2020) to relevant parties who need this information).

Relevant parties may include parents of children referred to or served by IDEA Part C, EIS programs and providers, childcare centers, staff in other locations where early intervention services are provided, early and regular Head Start and preschool programs, hospitals, and primary referral sources such as physicians, shelters, foster care programs, etc. Other activities that relate to service provision, including the provision of service coordination, evaluations, and assessments, may also continue to be funded.

When expending Part C funds, State LAs must follow the same policies and procedures they use when expending and accounting for their non-Federal funds, consistent with the Office of Management and Budget (OMB) Uniform Administrative Requirements, Cost Principles, and Audit Requirements for Federal Awards (Uniform Guidance) under 2 C.F.R. §§ 200.302(a) and 200.317.

Q2. Can State LAs and EIS providers use IDEA Part C funds to ensure the continuity of early intervention services through telecommunications or other methods during the COVID-19 pandemic?

Yes, in order to ensure the continuity of service coordination and early intervention services to infants and toddlers with disabilities and their families, State LAs and EIS providers may use IDEA Part C funds to provide early intervention services and service coordination services by initiating or expanding the use of telecommunications (e.g. telephone, video conferencing, or other methods).[28] The provision of services by alternate means during the COVID-19 pandemic does not mean that all early intervention services must be provided in this manner once a service can be provided in person when feasible, safe, and appropriate to do so and in-person service delivery is acceptable to the child's family. IDEA Part C funds can be used to support activities during the transition to in-person services.

Q3. What are other ways that State LAs and EIS providers can ensure continuity of services using IDEA Part C funds during the COVID-19 pandemic?

State LAs may use IDEA Part C funds for interim payments pending reimbursement from the agency or entity that has ultimate responsibility for the payment consistent with IDEA Part C payor of last resort requirements under 34 C.F.R. § 303.510(b) to prevent a delay in the timely provision of appropriate early intervention services.

This may be necessary as many States use a variety of funding sources for early intervention services, including public insurance and benefits and private insurance and the authorities (laws, regulations, State Medicaid plans, etc.) and billing systems around these funding sources are being revised to allow for payment for telecommunications as a result of the COVID-19 pandemic.

Q4. How are State LAs able to use IDEA Part C funds to increase their capacity to provide early intervention services remotely including by purchasing equipment?

During the COVID-19 pandemic, State LAs and local EIS providers and programs may need to purchase equipment and related assistive technology to continue the provision of appropriate early intervention services (including service coordination) for eligible infants and toddlers with disabilities and their families.

If those related equipment expenditures fall within the scope of the prior approval provided in OSERS's October 29, 2019, Frequently Asked Questions (FAQ) on Prior Approval for OSEP and RSA Formula Grants, State LAs are not required to submit prior approval requests for the equipment (defined generally as $5,000 or more per item of equipment). Under that prior approval FAQ document, grantees no longer need to submit prior approval requests under 34 C.F.R. § 303.104(a) to OSEP for equipment that is to be charged to IDEA funds and which is identified on, or directly related to the implementation of, Individualized Family Service Plans (IFSPs) assistive technology devices and other equipment needed to provide services on the IFSP.

However, if a State LA must purchase equipment that is not identified on or needed to implement the IFSP, then the State LA must submit a detailed prior approval request to OSEP and may submit that request electronically.

---

28. Use of telecommunications technology as a mechanism to provide service coordination and early intervention services, including home visits for infants and toddlers with disabilities and their families, are sometimes referred to as telehealth, tele-intervention, tele-therapy, and tele practice.

In reviewing requests for prior approval under 34 C.F.R. § 303.104(a), if OSEP determines that an IDEA Part C program will be improved by permitting IDEA Part C funds to be used to acquire the equipment, OSEP is authorized to allow the use of IDEA Part C funds for those purposes.

OSEP has streamlined its current approval process to respond to the anticipated increase in requests. When expending IDEA Part C funds, State LAs must follow the same policies and procedures they use for procurements from their non-Federal funds, consistent with the OMB Uniform Guidance for procurement under 2 C.F.R. § 200.317.[29]

---

29. In addition, State LAs must use, manage, and dispose of equipment in accordance with State laws and procedures, consistent with 2 C.F.R. § 200.313(b) and maintain appropriate records and cost documentation as required by 2 C.F.R. § 200.302 (financial management), 2 C.F.R. § 200.333 (retention requirements for records), and 2 C.F.R. § 200.430(i) (standards for documenting personnel expenses). Further, costs incurred that are associated with the COVID-19 pandemic will be allowable only if they are reasonable, necessary, and allocable to the grant, consistent with the Federal cost principles described in the OMB Uniform Guidance (2 C.F.R. §§ 200.403, 200.404, and 200.405), adequately documented (2 C.F.R. § 200.403(g)), and are consistent with the IDEA use of funds do not conflict with the applicable statutory and regulatory provisions. For guidance on the use of Federal funds to pay for the compensation of employees and for conference, training and travel related expenses, see Fact Sheet: Select Questions Related to Use of Department of Education Grant Funds during the Novel Coronavirus Disease 2019.

2.2.8

UNITED STATES DEPARTMENT OF EDUCATION

OFFICE OF SPECIAL EDUCATION AND REHABILITATIVE SERVICES
OFFICE OF SPECIAL EDUCATION PROGRAMS

June 26, 2020

The Office of Special Education Programs (OSEP), within the U.S. Department of Education's (Department) Office of Special Education and Rehabilitative Services, issues this Question and Answer (Q & A) document in response to inquiries concerning flexibility in the implementation of the Individuals with Disabilities Education Act (IDEA) Part B fiscal requirements in the current COVID-19 environment.

This Q & A document does not impose any additional requirements beyond those included in applicable law and regulations. It does not create or confer any rights for or on any person. The responses presented in this document generally constitute informal guidance representing the interpretation of the Department of the applicable statutory or regulatory requirements in the context of the specific facts presented here and are not legally binding and does not establish a policy or rule that would apply in all circumstances.

To review other Q & A documents that OSEP has provided related to COVID-19, please visit https://sites.ed.gov/idea/topic-areas/#COVID-19. Additional information specific to the COVID-19 pandemic may be found online at https://www.ed.gov/coronavirus.

FLEXIBILITY ON IDEA PART B FISCAL REQUIREMENTS

Q1. In light of the COVID-19 pandemic, we are anticipating that State revenues will be reduced and that there may be budget cuts in education generally, and special education specifically. Is there any flexibility in meeting the requirements for the maintenance of State financial support (MFS)?

Yes. As you know, under 34 C.F.R. § 300.163(a), a State must not reduce the amount of State financial support for special education and related services for children with disabilities, or otherwise made available because of the excess costs of educating those children, below the amount of that support for the preceding fiscal year. However, under 34 C.F.R. § 300.163(c), the Secretary may waive the MFS requirement for a State, for one fiscal year at a time, if the Secretary determines that—

1. Granting a waiver would be equitable due to exceptional or uncontrollable circumstances such as a natural disaster or a precipitous and unforeseen decline in the financial resources of the State; or
2. The State meets the standard in 34 C.F.R. § 300.164 for a waiver of the requirement to supplement, and not to supplant, funds received under Part B of IDEA.

Additional information about MFS waivers is posted on https://www2.ed.gov/policy/speced/guid/idea/monitor/smfs-partbwaivers.html.

In addition, States may establish compliance with the MFS requirement on a total or a per capita basis, and may switch between the two methods, but must establish compliance by applying the same method to the relevant comparison years (i.e., States establish compliance in a given year by showing that either:

1. the total dollar amount was at least equal to the total dollar amount of the previous year, OR
2. the per capita amount was at least equal to the per capita amount of the previous year).

Q2. Disruptions to services and school closures related to the COVID-19 pandemic have had a significant impact on the funds our local educational agencies (LEAs) have expended on the education of children with disabilities and may impact the amount they can budget for the upcoming year. Is there any flexibility in how LEAs meet the maintenance of effort (MOE) requirements?

Yes. LEAs may meet the MOE eligibility and compliance standards by using any of the following four methods:

1. total amount of State and local funds;
2. State and local funds on a per capita basis;
3. total amount of local funds only; or
4. local funds only on a per capita basis. See 34 C.F.R. § 300.203(a)(1) and (b)(2). The local funds only method, on either a total or a per capita basis, is an option LEAs may want to consider using to meet the MOE requirement if State funds available for the education of children with disabilities are reduced.[30]

---

30. More information on LEA MOE is available in <u>Office of Special Education Programs (OSEP) Memorandum 15-10</u>, Issuance of Guidance on the Final LEA MOE Regulations under Part B of the IDEA (July 27, 2015).

- Under 34 C.F.R. § 300.204, there are five allowable exceptions to the LEA MOE requirement. An LEA may reduce the level of expenditures for the education of children with disabilities below the level of those expenditures for the preceding fiscal year (for the compliance standard) and below the level of those expenditures for the most recent fiscal year for which information is available (for the eligibility standard), if the reduction is attributable to any of the following:
  a. The voluntary departure, by retirement or otherwise, or departure for just cause, of special education or related services personnel.
  b. A decrease in the enrollment of children with disabilities.
  c. The termination of the obligation of the agency, consistent with Part B of IDEA, to provide a program of special education to a particular child with a disability that is an exceptionally costly program, as determined by the State educational agency (SEA), because the child (1) has left the jurisdiction of the agency; (2) has reached the age at which the agency's obligation to provide a free appropriate public education to the child has terminated; or (3) no longer needs the program of special education.
  d. The termination of costly expenditures for long-term purchases, such as the acquisition of equipment or the construction of school facilities.
  e. The assumption of cost by the high cost fund operated by the SEA under 34 C.F.R. § 300.704(c).

In addition, under 34 C.F.R. § 300.205, for any fiscal year for which an LEA's IDEA section 611 allocation exceeds the amount the LEA received for the previous fiscal year, the LEA may reduce the level of expenditures for the education of children with disabilities otherwise required by 34 C.F.R. § 300.203(b) by not more than 50 percent of the amount of that excess. However, the maximum amount of expenditures the LEA may reduce under 34 C.F.R. § 300.205 is affected by the amount of funds expended by the LEA for coordinated early intervening services under 34 C.F.R. § 300.226. See 34 C.F.R. §§ 300.205(d) and 300.226(a); and Appendix D to 34 C.F.R. Part 300.

Finally, if an LEA fails to meet the MOE compliance standard, the SEA is liable in a recovery action under section 452 of the General Education Provisions Act (20 U.S.C. 1234a) to return to the Department, using non-Federal funds, an amount equal to the amount by which the LEA failed to maintain its level of expenditures in that fiscal year, or the amount of the LEA's IDEA Part B subgrant in that fiscal year, whichever is lower. 34 C.F.R. § 300.203(d). To the extent permitted under State law, the SEA may seek reimbursement of this amount from the LEA that did not meet the MOE compliance standard. Whether a State seeks recovery from an LEA is at the discretion of the State.

Q3. Because of the potential budget cuts and school closures during the COVID-19 pandemic, our LEAs are concerned they may not meet the excess cost requirement. Is there any flexibility in meeting this requirement under IDEA?

No. Excess costs means those costs that are in excess of the average annual per pupil expenditure (APPE) in an LEA during the preceding school year for an elementary school or secondary school student, as may be appropriate, and that must be computed in accordance with 34 C.F.R. § 300.16. To meet the excess cost requirement, an LEA must spend at least the APPE on the education of each student with a disability

- calculated separately at the elementary school level and the secondary school level
- before using IDEA Part B funds to pay for the excess costs of providing special education and related services to students with disabilities. If an LEA expends less funds on the education of all students (including students with disabilities), and if the APPE is then reduced, the amount the LEA must expend on students with disabilities to meet the excess cost requirement would also be reduced. See also 34 C.F.R. § 300.202(b) and Appendix A to 34 C.F.R. Part 300.

2.2.9

UNITED STATES DEPARTMENT OF EDUCATION

OFFICE OF SPECIAL EDUCATION AND REHABILITATIVE SERVICES
OFFICE OF SPECIAL EDUCATION PROGRAMS

June 30, 2020

The Office of Special Education Programs (OSEP), within the U.S. Department of Education's (Department) Office of Special Education and Rehabilitative Services, issues this Question and Answer (Q & A) document in response to inquiries concerning implementation of the Individuals with Disabilities Education Act (IDEA) Part B procedural safeguards in the current COVID-19 environment.

This Q & A document does not impose any additional requirements beyond those included in applicable law and regulations. It does not create or confer any rights for or on any person. The responses presented in this document generally constitute informal guidance representing the interpretation of the Department of the applicable statutory or regulatory requirements in the context of the specific facts presented here and are not legally binding and does not establish a policy or rule that would apply in all circumstances.

To review other Q & A documents that OSEP has provided related to COVID-19, please visit https://sites.ed.gov/idea/topic-areas/#COVID-19. Additional information specific to the COVID-19 pandemic may be found online at https://www.ed.gov/coronavirus.

IDEA PART B PROCEDURAL SAFEGUARDS

Parental Consent

Q1. May a public agency accept an electronic or digital signature to indicate that the parent consents to their child's initial evaluation, reevaluation, or the initial provision of special education and related services to their child?

Yes, so long as the public agency ensures there are appropriate safeguards in place to protect the integrity of the process. IDEA requires public agencies to obtain informed consent from the parent of the child, consistent with 34 C.F.R. § 300.9, before conducting an initial evaluation and a reevaluation of a child, subject to certain exceptions, and before the initial provision of special education and related services to the child. 34 C.F.R. § 300.300. Under 34 C.F.R. § 300.9, consent, which must be voluntary on the part of the parent, means the parent has been fully informed of, and agrees in writing to the activity for which his or her consent has been requested. Because of social distancing and other restrictions during the pandemic, it may not be possible to obtain a parent's signed, written consent in person.

In developing appropriate safeguards for using electronic or digital signatures during the pandemic, a public agency may determine that a "signed and dated written consent" may include a record and signature in electronic form that identifies and authenticates a particular person as the source of the consent and indicates such person's approval of the information contained in the electronic consent. See 34 C.F.R. § 99.30(d) (consent for disclosure of personally identifiable information (PII) from education records).

> These safeguards also should include a statement that indicates that the parent has been fully informed of the relevant activity and that the consent is voluntary on the part of the parent consistent with the IDEA definition of "consent" in 34 C.F.R. § 300.9. During the pandemic, the Department considers the use of these safeguards to be sufficient for public agencies to use in accepting electronic signatures for parental consent under IDEA for the activities described above.

Q2. May a public agency accept a parent's electronic or digital signature as written parental consent to disclose PII from the child's education records?

Yes, so long as the safeguards described in Q1 above are applied and met. That is, electronic signatures for consent may be accepted to satisfy the IDEA Part B consent requirements for disclosure of PII from education records if there are appropriate safeguards, which could include the use of the safeguards for granting consent electronically to release PII from education records described in the response to Q1 above. 34 C.F.R. § 99.30(d).

In addition, under 34 C.F.R. 300.9, consent, which must be voluntary on the part of the parent, means the parent has been fully informed of, and agrees in writing to the activity for which his or her consent has been requested. Parental consent must be obtained before PII is disclosed to parties other than officials of participating agencies or unless a specific exception applies under 34 C.F.R. § 300.622(b) of the IDEA Part B regulations or under the Family Educational Rights and Privacy Act (FERPA) and its implementing regulations at 34 C.F.R. Part 99.[31] 34 C.F.R. § 300.622. In addition, under Part B of IDEA, these safeguards should include a statement that indicates that the parent has been fully informed of the relevant activity and that the consent is voluntary on the part of the parent consistent with the IDEA definition of "consent" in 34 C.F.R. § 300.9.

---

31. For further information regarding consent for disclosure of PII, see Understanding the Confidentiality Requirements Applicable to IDEA Early Childhood Programs Frequently Asked Questions (October 2016).

IDEA Part B also requires that prior to accessing a child's or parent's public benefits or insurance for the first time and after providing the annual notification to parents consistent with 34 C.F.R. § 300.154(d)(2)(v), the public agency must obtain written consent from the parent that meets the requirements of 34 C.F.R. §§ 99.30 and 300.622, for disclosure of PII from education records to a State's public benefits or insurance program (e.g., Medicaid) in order for the public agency to bill that State's program for services provided under 34 C.F.R. Part 300. 34 C.F.R. § 300.154(d)(2)(iv).

Prior Written Notice

Q3. How can a public agency provide parents with prior written notice required under 34 C.F.R. § 300.503, while school buildings and other public agency facilities are closed due to the pandemic?

A public agency must provide parents written notice a reasonable time before it proposes or refuses to initiate or change the identification, evaluation, educational placement of the child, or the provision of a free appropriate public education (FAPE) to the child. 34 C.F.R. § 300.503. If the parent has previously agreed, or agrees during the pandemic, the prior written notice can be provided through electronic mail (email). 34 C.F.R. § 300.505.

The term "reasonable time" is not defined in the regulation. The Department believes that it would be appropriate to consider factors such as the closure of public and school buildings and facilities, social distancing, and other health-related orders during the pandemic in determining what constitutes a reasonable time for this purpose. Nevertheless, public agencies should make every effort to ensure that written notice is provided as soon as possible prior to the proposed or refused action.

The determination of when prior written notice is required depends on the particular facts and circumstances, but OSEP encourages public agencies to ensure that parents are fully informed of how their child's special education and related services needs are addressed during remote learning.

Procedural Safeguards Notice

Q4. Given the challenges associated with school operations during the pandemic, how can a public agency ensure that a copy of the procedural safeguards available to parents under IDEA is provided in accordance with 34 C.F.R. § 300.504(a)?

The public agency can provide a parent an electronic copy of the procedural safeguards notice (e.g., through email) instead of a paper copy, if the parent has previously agreed, or agrees to receive an electronic copy during the pandemic. See 34 C.F.R. § 300.505. The public agency must provide the parents a copy of the procedural safeguards available to the parents of a child with a disability only one time a school year, except that the notice also must be provided to parents in the circumstances specified in 34 C.F.R. § 300.504(a). The public agency is not required to provide a parent an electronic or paper copy of the notice of procedural safeguards if the parent declines a copy upon being offered a copy.

The public agency should document that it offered the parent a copy and that the parent declined.

Access to Education Records

Q5. How can a public agency comply with a parent's request to inspect and review the child's education records[32] while school buildings and other public facilities are closed due to the pandemic?

In light of the social distancing and physical contact restrictions of many jurisdictions during the pandemic, parents and public agencies may identify a mutually agreeable timeframe and method to provide access to the child's education records. If the parent asks to inspect and review specific documents from the child's education records while school buildings are closed during the pandemic, the school and parent should work together to identify mutually agreeable options for access to the education records. For example, the school could provide the parent with the requested information from the child's records via email, a secure on-line portal, or postal mail until school reopens. Note though, the public agency must use reasonable methods when transmitting PII in education records through email or an online portal.[33] See FERPA and Virtual Learning During COVID-19.

---

32. The IDEA provisions related to access rights require that a participating agency comply with a parent's request to inspect and review their child's education records without unnecessary delay, before any meeting regarding an Individualized education program, or any due process hearing or a resolution session, and in no case more than 45 days after the request has been made. 34 C.F.R. § 300.613. Under FERPA and its implementing regulations, the educational agency or institution must comply with a request for access to records within a reasonable period of time, but not more than 45 days after it has received the request. 34 C.F.R. § 99.10.

33. Also see OSEP Letter to Breton (March 21, 2014)

2.2.10

UNITED STATES DEPARTMENT OF EDUCATION

OFFICE OF SPECIAL EDUCATION AND REHABILITATIVE SERVICES
OFFICE OF SPECIAL EDUCATION PROGRAMS

June 30, 2020

The Office of Special Education Programs (OSEP), within the U.S. Department of Education's (Department) Office of Special Education and Rehabilitative Services, issues this Question and Answer (Q & A) document in response to inquiries concerning implementation of the Individuals with Disabilities Education Act (IDEA) Part C procedural safeguards in the current COVID-19 environment.

This Q & A document does not impose any additional requirements beyond those included in applicable law and regulations. It does not create or confer any rights for or on any person. The responses presented in this document generally constitute informal guidance representing the interpretation of the Department of the applicable statutory or regulatory requirements in the context of the specific facts presented here and are not legally binding and does not establish a policy or rule that would apply in all circumstances.

To review other Q & A documents that OSEP has provided related to COVID-19, please visit https://sites.ed.gov/idea/topic-areas/#COVID-19. Additional information specific to the COVID-19 pandemic may be found online at https://www.ed.gov/coronavirus.

IDEA PART C PROCEDURAL SAFEGUARDS

Parental Consent

Q1. May a State Lead Agency (State LA) or early intervention service (EIS) provider accept an electronic or digital signature to indicate that the parent provides consent under Part C of the IDEA (when required for screening if a State has opted to offer screening, the evaluation, assessment, provision of early intervention services, disclosure of personally identifiable information (PII), or the use of benefits or insurance for their infant or toddler)?

Yes, so long as the State LA or EIS provider ensures there are appropriate safeguards for the parental consent required under Part C of IDEA under 34 C.F.R. § 303.7. The lead agency may, but is not required to, accept an electronic or digital signature provided it adopts the appropriate safeguards. OSEP has previously advised that these safeguards include that the electronic signature:

1. is signed and dated;
2. identifies and authenticates a particular person as the source of the electronic consent;
3. indicates such person's approval of the information contained in the electronic consent; and
4. is accompanied by a statement that the person understands and agrees.[34]

IDEA requires State LAs and EIS providers to obtain informed written consent from parents, consistent with 34 C.F.R. § 303.7 for their child's screening (in States that have adopted screening procedures), evaluations and assessments, and before the provision of early intervention services, including before the initiation of each early intervention service. Parental consent is also required before the disclosure of PII under certain circumstances in accordance with 34 C.F.R. § 303.414 or prior to the use of public benefits or insurance or private insurance in certain circumstances in accordance with 34 C.F.R. § 303.520 and 34 C.F.R. § 303.420(a)(1)–(4) Because of social distancing and other restrictions during the pandemic, it may not be possible to obtain a parent's signed, written consent in person.

Q2. May the State LA or EIS provider accept a parent's electronic or digital signature as written parental consent to disclose PII from the child's early intervention records?

Yes, so long as the safeguards described in Q1 above are applied and met. These safeguards include that the electronic signature:

1. is signed and dated;
2. identifies and authenticates a particular person as the source of the electronic consent;
3. indicates such person's approval of the information contained in the electronic consent; and
4. is accompanied by a statement that the person understands and agrees.

Parental consent must be obtained before PII is disclosed to parties other than authorized representatives, officials, or employees of participating agencies (which includes the State LA and EIS provider) unless a specific exception applies under 34 C.F.R. § 303.414(b) of the IDEA Part C regulations, which incorporates the exceptions under the Family Educational Rights and Privacy Act (FERPA) regulations in 34 C.F.R. Part 99.31.[35]

---

34. 34 C.F.R. 303.7; also see OSEP Letter to Greer (July 19, 2013)
35. For further information regarding consent for disclosure of PII, see Understanding the Confidentiality Requirements Applicable to IDEA Early Childhood Programs Frequently Asked Questions (October 2016).

Prior Written Notice and Procedural Safeguards Notice

Q3. How can a State LA or EIS provider provide the prior written notice required under 34 C.F.R. § 303.421, while agencies and other facilities are closed due to the pandemic?

If the parent has previously agreed, or agrees during the pandemic, the prior written notice and procedural safeguards notice can be provided through electronic mail (email). The State LA or EIS provider must provide parents written notice a reasonable time before it proposes or refuses to initiate or change the identification, evaluation, or placement of their infant or toddler, or the provision of early intervention services to the infant or toddler with a disability and his or her family. 34 C.F.R § 303.421. The prior written notice must include information regarding all procedural safeguards that are available under Part C. 34 C.F.R. § 303.421.

The term "reasonable time" is not defined in the regulation. The Department believes that it would be appropriate to consider factors such as the closure of agencies and public facilities such as schools, social distancing, and other health-related orders during the pandemic in determining what constitutes a reasonable time for this purpose. Nevertheless, the State LA or EIS provider should make every effort to ensure that written notice is provided as soon as possible prior to the proposed or refused action.

The determination of when prior written notice is required will depend on the particular facts and circumstances, but OSEP encourages State LAs and EIS providers to ensure that parents are fully informed of how their infant's or toddler's early intervention service needs are addressed during the time that IDEA Part C services are provided remotely.

Access to Early Intervention Records

Q4. How can a State LA or EIS provider comply with a parent's request to inspect and review the infant's or toddler's early intervention records[36] while agencies and other public facilities are closed due to the pandemic?

In light of the social distancing and physical contact restrictions of many jurisdictions during the pandemic, parents and State LAs and EIS providers may identify a mutually agreeable timeframe and method for providing access to the infant's or toddler's early intervention records. If the parent asks to inspect and review specific documents from the infant's or toddler's early intervention records while agencies and public facilities are closed during the pandemic, State LA staff, EIS providers, and the parent should work together to identify mutually agreeable options to provide access to the early intervention records.

---

36. Each participating agency must permit parents of a child referred to, or served under Part C, to inspect and review all early intervention records relating to their child and family. Under IDEA, the agency must comply with a request without unnecessary delay, and before any individualized family service plan (IFSP) team meeting, or a due process hearing, or a resolution session (if the Lead Agency has adopted Part B due process hearing procedures) and, in no case more than 10 days after the request has been made. 34 C.F.R. § 303.405.

For example, the State LA or EIS provider could provide the parent with the requested information from the infant's or toddler's records via email, a secure on-line portal, or postal mail until the State LA or EIS provider offices reopen. Note though, the State LA or EIS provider must use reasonable methods when transmitting PII in early intervention records through email or an on-line portal. See FERPA and Virtual Learning During COVID-19.

2.2.11

UNITED STATES DEPARTMENT OF EDUCATION

OFFICE OF SPECIAL EDUCATION AND REHABILITATIVE SERVICES
OFFICE OF SPECIAL EDUCATION PROGRAMS

July 6, 2020

The Office of Special Education Programs (OSEP), within the U.S. Department of Education's (Department) Office of Special Education and Rehabilitative Services, issues this Question and Answer (Q & A) document in response to inquiries concerning implementation of the Individuals with Disabilities Education Act (IDEA) Part C evaluation and assessment timelines in the current COVID-19 environment.

This Q & A document does not impose any additional requirements beyond those included in applicable law and regulations. It does not create or confer any rights for or on any person. The responses presented in this document generally constitute informal guidance representing the interpretation of the Department of the applicable statutory or regulatory requirements in the context of the specific facts presented here and are not legally binding and does not establish a policy or rule that would apply in all circumstances.

To review other Q & A documents that OSEP has provided related to COVID-19, please visit https://sites.ed.gov/idea/topic-areas/#COVID-19. Additional information specific to the COVID-19 pandemic may be found online at https://www.ed.gov/coronavirus.

INITIAL EVALUATION AND ASSESSMENT TIMELINE

IDEA Part C requires a timely, comprehensive, multidisciplinary evaluation to determine the eligibility of each child, birth through age two, who is referred for an evaluation or early intervention services and suspected of having a disability. If the child is determined eligible, an assessment is conducted to determine the appropriate early intervention services and supports for the child and family.

Q1. What exceptions are available to a State Lead Agency (State LA) and its early intervention service (EIS) providers in meeting the 45-day timeline requirement for conducting initial evaluations and assessments and Individualized Family Service Plan (IFSP) meetings when access to homes and facilities are limited or have restrictions that prevent face-to-face meetings?

The IDEA Part C 45-day timeline is in 34 C.F.R. §§ 303.310, 303.342(a) and 303.345(c). The 45-day timeline applies to:

1. any screening offered by the State,
2. the initial evaluation,
3. the initial child and family assessment, and
4. the initial Individualized IFSP meeting.

This timeline requirement includes two allowable exceptions:

1. The child or parent is unavailable to complete the screening (if applicable), the initial evaluation, the initial assessments of the child and family, or the initial IFSP meeting due to exceptional family circumstances that are documented in the child's early intervention records; or
2. The parent has not provided consent for the screening (if applicable), the initial evaluation, or the initial assessment of the child, despite documented, repeated attempts by the State LA or EIS provider to obtain parental consent.

OSEP has historically also applied this documented "exceptional family circumstances" exception when clear circumstances outside the State LA's or EIS provider's control, such as a hurricane, do not permit the underlying activity to occur and thus the child and family are unavailable as a practical matter.[37] In these very limited circumstances, under 34 C.F.R. § 303.310(c), the State LA or EIS provider must:

1. document in the child's early intervention record the exceptional family circumstances; and
2. complete the activities as soon as possible after the documented exceptional family circumstances no longer exist.

The Department acknowledges that it may not be possible to complete some or any of the activities required within the 45-day timeline remotely. For example, conducting an in-person observation may be critical to ensuring appropriate evaluation and assessment. Given that in-person meetings may not be feasible or advisable due to the COVID-19 pandemic, such restrictions can constitute a documented exceptional family circumstance that qualifies for an exception to the 45-day timeline. In these situations, the State LA or EIS provider must document application of the exception in the child's early intervention record, and complete the delayed evaluation, assessment, or initial IFSP as soon possible after the exceptional circumstances no longer exist. Determinations regarding whether

---

37. Note that this exception does not apply if the State LA or EIS provider staff are unavailable due to staffing shortages, etc.

an exceptional family circumstance exists must be made on a case by-case basis. The 45-day timeline cannot be extended for all children within a state under the assumption that COVID-19 is an exceptional family circumstance for all families.

INTERIM IFSP

Q2. Can the State LAs and their local EIS providers use the interim IFSP until a face-to-face evaluation(s) or meeting(s) can be held?

Yes. An interim IFSP may be helpful when an initial IFSP cannot be developed and the parents and State LA or EIS providers agree on the IFSP services needed by the eligible child and family. The Department wants to highlight the use of "interim IFSPs" where documented exceptional family circumstances caused a delay in completing the initial evaluation and assessments during the 45-day timeline requirement.

Any early intervention services that have been determined to be needed by, and that can be available immediately to, the child and the child's family, particularly those which can be provided remotely (particularly during the pandemic when in-person meetings are limited), with parental consent, may begin before the completion of the evaluation or assessments.

CONDUCTING AN EVALUATION AND ASSESSMENT

Q3. How can a State LA or its EIS providers conduct evaluations to determine a child's eligibility for IDEA Part C or conduct the child assessment when staff cannot conduct in-person meetings or conduct home visits due to the pandemic?

The Department acknowledges that social distancing measures and other limitations during the pandemic may make administering most in-person evaluations impracticable and may place limitations on how evaluations and the child assessment are conducted under IDEA Part C. Thus, the Department highlights the option of using medical records, when appropriate, to establish eligibility without conducting an evaluation. When using medical records to establish eligibility, the State LA or EIS provider must still conduct an appropriate assessment of the child and a family-directed assessment.

State LAs may wish to investigate available assessment instruments and tools to determine if some can be administered or completed remotely during the pandemic, provided that assessment of the child is based on personal observation (whether in person or through videoconferencing). State LAs may also work with the developers of their current assessment instruments to determine if the instruments can be administered or completed remotely, without significantly impacting the validity of the results.

An interim IFSP may be put into place with parental consent under 34 C.F.R. § 303.345 to provide IDEA Part C services before the evaluation or assessment is completed, and in addition must include the name of the responsible service coordinator, consistent with 34 C.F.R. § 303.344(g). The service coordinator will implement the interim IFSP and coordinate with any other agencies or people as appropriate.

The requirements for an interim IFSP are in 34 C.F.R. §§ 303.310(c) and 303.345.

The option to use medical records when determining eligibility are in 34 C.F.R. § 303.321(a)(3)(i).

The provider must still conduct an appropriate assessment[38] of the child and a family directed assessment.[39]

State LAs may wish to investigate available assessment instruments and tools to determine if some can be administered or completed remotely during the pandemic, provided that assessment of the child is based on personal observation (whether in person or through videoconferencing). State LAs may also work with the developers of their current assessment instruments to determine if the instruments can be administered or completed remotely, without significantly impacting the validity of the results.

---

38. The assessment of the child must include: a review of the results of the evaluation, personal observations of the child, and identification of the child's needs in each of the development areas. 34 C.F.R. § 303.321(c)(1).
39. The family directed-assessment must, among other requirements, be based on information obtained through an assessment tool and through an interview of appropriate family members. 34 C.F.R. § 303.321(c)(2).

CHAPTER 3

A Primer on Dispute Resolution Under the IDEA and Section 504

The Individuals with Disabilities Education Act (IDEA) contains mechanisms by which parents and school district administrators can settle disputes regarding the special education of students with disabilities. Two avenues of dispute resolution are particularly germane to our purposes in this textbook: the State Education Agency's (SEA) complaint resolution process (CRP) and the due process hearing (DPH). We will not cover two other dispute resolution mechanisms included in the IDEA—mediation, and the resolution session—because they are less formal and are mechanisms to resolve disputes before they reach the level of the DPH.

3.1 Dispute Resolution

The purposes of the state CRP and the DPH are similar (i.e., to resolve disputes regarding an IDEA-eligible student's special education), but the ways the two systems operate are significantly different. Zirkel (2020) describes the CRP system as investigative and the DPH system as adjudicative. We next describe the two systems of dispute resolution.

3.1.1 State complaint resolution

Regulations to the IDEA require that each state adopt a procedure whereby a student's parents can file a complaint against a school district regarding the special education provided to their child.[1] A student's parents or any other person or organization, except for a student's school district, may file a complaint with the SEA. The complaint must be filed within one year of the date on which the violation occurred, although states may extend this timeline. When the complaint is received, officials in the SEA must investigate the allegations.

---

1. Regulations to the IDEA addressing the state complaint system may be found at 34 C.F.R. § 300.151 to 300.153.

The school district being investigated must also be given an opportunity to respond to the parents' allegations and the parents must be given an opportunity to amend their complaint. If SEA officials determine a formal investigation is needed, an on-site investigation will be conducted in the district.

After the complaint is filed the SEA has sixty days for officials to issue a written decision in which they (a) provide the details of their independent determination, (b) present their findings of facts and conclusions, and (c) give their rationale for arriving at their decision. If it is found that a school district failed to provide appropriate services, the SEA report must describe the district's failure, include corrective actions that address a student's needs (e.g., compensatory services), and detail the actions the school district should take to prevent similar situations from occurring in the future.

The SEA's CRP may be preferred by some parents because attorneys are not required, final decisions are usually made more quickly, and it is less financially and emotionally taxing (Zirkel, 2020). Additionally, the CRP process requires little involvement of a student's parents. Moreover, Zirkel asserts, CRPs tend to issue rulings in parents' favor more frequently than in the DPH mechanism. The CRP mechanism does not include the right to confront and cross-examine witnesses, and there is no mandated right to appeal the decision to the SEA, unless the right exists in the laws of the state in which the CRP is conducted.

According to comments about the 2006 regulations to the IDEA, there is no federally guaranteed right to judicial review of the CRP decision.

> The regulations neither prohibit nor require the establishment of procedures to permit an LEA or other party to request reconsideration of a State complaint decision. We have chosen to be silent in the regulations about whether a State complaint decision may be appealed because we believe States are in the best position to determine what, if any, appeals process is necessary to meet each State's needs, consistent with State law (IDEA Regulations Comments, 2006, p. 46607).

If a student's parents do not agree with the finding in the CRP, they may file for a DPH. The ruling of the DPH may be appealed to a state or federal court.

3.1.2 The Due Process Hearing

The DPH is the most well known of the IDEA's dispute solution systems.[2] Although either parents or school district officials may file for a DPH, requests for hearings are more commonly brought by a student's parents. School officials or parents may file for a DPH within two years of when the parents knew or should have known of a violation (34 C.F.R. 300.507[a][2]). Note that states may set their own time frame regarding the statute of limitations. Additionally, dispute resolution under Section 504 is the same as is required under the IDEA. Unlike the IDEA, however, Section 504 puts the responsibility for all DPHs on the local educational agency (LEA).

---

2. Regulations to the IDEA addressing the state complaint system may be found at 34 C.F.R. § 300.507 to 300.516.

An impartial hearing officer (IHO) presides over a DPH. The IHO cannot be employed by a school district or by the SEA involved in the education of the student or have any personal or professional interest that could interfere with his or her objectivity (34. C.F.R. § 300.511[c]). The IHO must understand state and federal laws and be able to render and write decisions using acceptable legal practices. The role of the IHO is to listen to the arguments of both sides and to apply the law to the specific facts of the case. The possible remedies an IHO may order include injunctive relief, compensatory education, and tuition reimbursement, but probably not attorney's fees.

The issues heard in a DPH may include any issue related to the identification, evaluation, or educational placement of a student with a disability, or the provision of FAPE to the student (34 C.F.R. 300.507[a]). Both parties in the DPH process have the rights that a litigant has in a hearing in a court, such as the right to (a) retain and be represented by an attorney, (b) present evidence, (c) examine and cross-examine witnesses, (d) obtain written or electronic verbatim record of the hearing and written or electronic records of the findings of fact and the decision (34 C.F.R. 300.512[a][1–5]). A DPH is very much like a court trial except that it is less formal. The decision must be made within forty-five days of the end of the hearing. The ruling of the IHO is final; however, either party has the right to appeal within ninety days of the final ruling. Note that these time lines can be different depending on state laws.

In most states, called one-tier states, the appeal of a DPH is made to a state or federal court. In a few states, called two-tier states, an appeal of a DPH ruling is made to the SEA, more specifically to a state review officer (SRO). The decision of the SEA can then be appealed to a state or federal court. Most appeals are to the federal courts, so we next examine appeals to these courts. Prior to filing an appeal, parents must exhaust their administrative remedies, which means in a one-tier state the parents must have gone through the DPH, and in a two-tier state the parents must have gone through the DPH and the state review. Usually, the only exception to the exhaustion requirement is when going through the procedures would be futile.

3.2 Special Education Disputes in the Federal Court System

The federal court system is a hierarchy. Figure 3.1 depicts the hierarchy of the federal courts. Similarly, state courts are also hierarchical (see Figure 3.2).

Figure 3.1 depicts the US district courts, the US circuit courts of appeals, and the US Supreme Court. Appeals of a ruling from the DPH go to the first level of federal courts, the US district court. Appeals from the US direct courts go to the US courts of appeals, also called the appellate or circuit courts, in its jurisdiction. The final appeal is to the US Supreme Court, the court of last resort.

3.2.1 The US district courts

The United States has ninety-four federal district courts. Every state has at least one district court, and some states have as many as four. In most circumstances

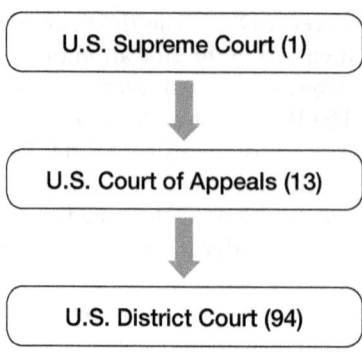

Figure 3.1 Federal Court System.

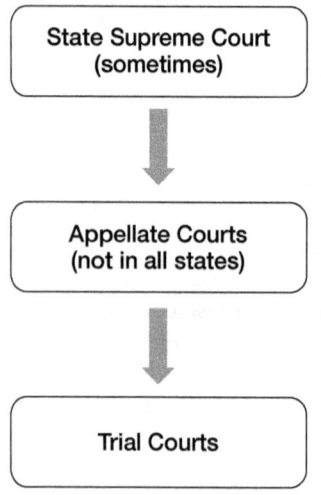

- State-level courts have the ability to resolve both state and federal claims
- State supreme court decisions can be appealed directly to the U.S. Supreme Court on issues of federal law.

Figure 3.2 Typical State Court System.

federal district courts, sometimes called trial courts, hear the facts of a case, apply the law, and issue a ruling. Often in the federal district court a jury will hear the facts of the case and issue a ruling. Juries are not present in special education cases brought under the IDEA.

When an IHO ruling is appealed to a US district court, however, the judge reviews the facts as determined by the IHO, determines if the IHO applied the law correctly, and either affirms or overturns the ruling of the IHO. In *Board of Education of the Hendrick Hudson Central School District v. Rowley* (1982), the US Supreme Court noted that the IDEA's requirement that a reviewing court receive the records from the administrative proceedings (i.e., the DPH) "carries the implied requirement that due weight shall be given to these proceedings"

(Rowley, 1982, p. 208). This means that the district court judge acts more as an appellate judge would act because unless the judge determines that the IHO made errors, the facts are considered fixed, and the judge determines if the IHO applied the law correctly. If a district court judge determines the IHO incorrectly determined the facts, the judge may review the case without giving deference to the IHO's ruling. This is referred to as hearing the case *de novo*, which means the district court judge decides the case without deferring to the IHO's ruling.[3]

Decisions from federal district courts do not create precedent outside of the district courts' jurisdiction. So, for example, a ruling from a US district court in South Carolina would not be binding on a US district court in Arkansas. Nonetheless, judges in the district court in Arkansas could certainly choose to follow the ruling of the district court in South Carolina if they found that ruling persuasive.

In an appeal of a ruling in a DPH to a federal district court, the attorneys for the parents and the school district will write arguments called briefs and submit them to the federal district court judge. The party that loses will typically claim the DPH was not conducted properly, the IHO misapplied the law, or both. The task of the federal court judge will be to determine if the IHO applied the law correctly. The judge will either affirm or overturn the ruling of the IHO. The losing party may then file an appeal with the next highest courts in the federal court hierarchy, the US courts of appeals.

3.2.2 The US courts of appeals

The next highest level of courts, immediately above the US district courts and immediately below the US Supreme Court, is the US circuit courts of appeals for the various circuits. The ninety-four US district court jurisdictions are divided into twelve judicial circuits.[4] Each of these circuits has an appellate court that hears appeals from the US district court. Table 3.1 depicts these jurisdictions and Figure 3.3 presents the geographic boundaries of the jurisdictions.

A US court of appeals hears appeals of rulings from the US district court in its jurisdiction. For example, the US court of appeals for the Fourth Circuit would hear appeals from the US district courts for Maryland, North Carolina, South Carolina, Virginia, and West Virginia because those states are in the Fourth Circuit. The US court of appeals for the Fourth Circuit would not hear cases from the US district court in Pennsylvania, however, because the Pennsylvania court is in the jurisdiction of the US court of appeals for the Third Circuit.

Rulings from the US courts of appeals set precedent for the lower courts within their jurisdictions. For example, a ruling from the US court of appeals for the Third Circuit will be binding on all the lower courts in the Third Circuit (i.e., the US district court for Delaware, New Jersey, Pennsylvania, and the Virgin Islands). On the other hand, rulings from the US court of appeals for the Third Circuit would not be binding on the US district court for the district of

---

3. *De novo* is from Latin and means "starting anew."
4. There is a thirteenth appellate court called the Court of Appeals for the Federal Circuit. This court has nationwide jurisdiction to hear specialized cases such as trademarks, patents, and international trade.

TABLE 3.1 **Circuit and District Court Jurisdictions.**

Circuit	Jurisdiction
First	Maine, Massachusetts, New Hampshire, Puerto Rico, Rhode Island
Second	Connecticut, New York, Vermont
Third	Delaware, New Jersey, Pennsylvania, Virgin Islands
Fourth	Maryland, North Carolina, South Carolina, Virginia, West Virginia
Fifth	Louisiana, Mississippi, Texas
Sixth	Kentucky, Ohio, Michigan, Tennessee
Seventh	Illinois, Indiana, Wisconsin
Eighth	Arkansas, Iowa, Minnesota, Missouri, Nebraska, North Dakota, South Dakota
Ninth	Alaska, Arizona, California, Guam, Hawaii, Idaho, Montana, Nevada, Northern Mariana Islands, Oregon, Washington
Tenth	Colorado, Kansas, New Mexico, Oklahoma, Utah, Wyoming
Eleventh	Alabama, Florida, Georgia
Twelfth (DC)	Washington, DC
Thirteenth (Federal)	Washington, DC (specialized courts)

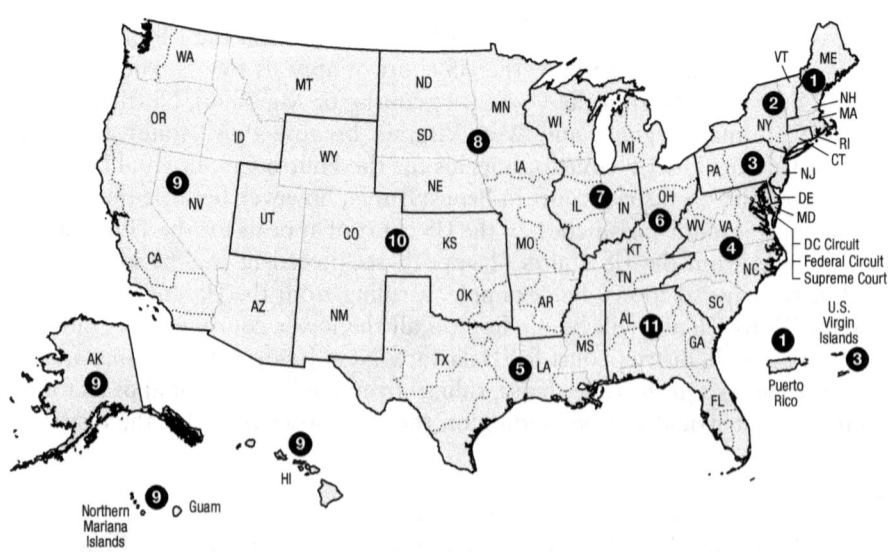

Figure 3.3 Boundaries of the US Courts of Appeals and the US District Court.

Arkansas because Arkansas is in the jurisdiction of the US court of appeals for the Eighth Circuit (i.e., the districts of Arkansas, Iowa, Minnesota, Missouri, Nebraska, North Dakota, and South Dakota). Because of the importance of the appellate courts, rulings from this level often have persuasive authority and are adopted by other courts in other jurisdictions even though they are not binding. An example of an appellate court ruling in special education that had great persuasive authority was *Daniel R. R. v. State Board of Education* (1989). Although the ruling of the US court of appeals for the Fifth Circuit only had binding or controlling authority on district courts in Louisiana, Mississippi, and Texas, the decision was eventually adopted by the US court of appeals for the Second Circuit (Connecticut, New York, Vermont), the US court of appeals for the Third Circuit (Delaware, New Jersey, Pennsylvania), the US court of appeals for the Tenth Circuit (Colorado, Kansas, Oklahoma, New Mexico, Utah, Wyoming), and the US court of appeals for the Eleventh Circuit (Alabama, Florida, Georgia).

Appellate courts do not have juries, hear witnesses, or retry cases. Rather, appellate courts review the procedures and rulings of the district courts and determine if the law was applied correctly. A US circuit court is comprised of several judges (the number of judges differs by circuit) divided into panels of three. Most cases appealed to the circuit courts will be heard and ruled on by these panels of three judges. Rarely, a case will be heard by all the judges on a court of appeals, a process called hearing a case en banc.[5] In an en banc hearing the full court makes the ruling. This typically occurs when the court believes a significant issue needs to be heard in this manner or when one or both parties requests an en banc hearing and the judges agree to it. In a case reviewed in this text out of the US court of appeals for the Fourth Circuit (*R.S. v. Board of Directors of Woods Charter School Company*, 2020), an appeal was made to have the case heard en banc. The appellate court decided not to hear the case en banc, so the ruling stood.

With respect to special education rulings, the attorneys for both sides will file briefs with the appellate court. Typically the losing party will contend that the district court judge did not apply the law correctly or, in the case of an overturned DPH ruling, that the district court judge did not properly consider the ruling by the IHO. A party that loses at the appellate level may file an appeal with the highest court in the land, the US Supreme Court.

3.2.3 The US Supreme Court

The US Supreme Court is the highest court in the land. Rulings from the Supreme Court are binding in all jurisdictions. Each year the Supreme Court receives approximately eight thousand appeals of rulings out of the US circuit courts of appeals. These appeals are called petitions for a writ of certiorari. This petition, typically written by attorneys for a party not satisfied with the decision of an appellate court, essentially asks the Supreme Court to request that a lower court send up records of a case for review. Often the Supreme Court will ask the solicitor general of the United States, the fourth highest-ranking official in the US Department of Justice, to file a brief in the case expressing the views of the US government.

---

5. *En banc* is a French term meaning "in the bench."

The petition will ask the court to answer a question or two of major importance in the case. The Supreme Court is not required to hear cases appealed to it. In fact, the Supreme Court grants certiorari and generally hears less than 1 percent of the cases appealed to it. Generally the US Supreme Court will hear cases of significance or cases that represent a split or disagreement among the circuits. If the Supreme Court justices decide to hear a case, called granting the petition for certiorari, the case is placed on the docket. Attorneys for the petitioner and respondent are then given a limited amount of time in which they are to write a brief limited to fifty pages. After the original briefs are filed, both parties may write shorter briefs responding to the written arguments of the other party. The US solicitor general will also file a brief representing the views of the federal government. Additionally, if the Supreme Court allows it, parties not directly involved with the case but who are nonetheless interested in its outcome may file friend-of-the-court briefs called amicus curiae. The Supreme Court will then schedule oral arguments. During oral arguments, the petitioner and the respondent have approximately thirty minutes each to present their case. Typically the justices will pepper the attorneys with questions during their presentations. After the allotted hour, oral arguments will end and the justices will proceed to conference to discuss the case. After the case has been decided, the senior justice in the majority will assign a justice to write the majority opinion. If a justice agrees with the outcome of the case but not the rationale for arriving at it, he or she may write a concurring opinion. Any justice who disagrees with the majority opinion may write a dissenting opinion.

The US Supreme Court has ruled on only twelve special education cases (thirteen if a decision that ended in a tie is counted). These cases are of tremendous importance to special educators throughout the United States because rulings by the Supreme Court are binding on all lower courts and DPHs in the country. The cases we review in this book are the highest federal court cases heard in the year 2020 regarding students with disabilities and federal law. The US Supreme Court heard no cases in 2020.

3.3 Published and Unpublished Decisions

Readers will notice some cases featured in this book are listed with a citation (e.g., 959 F.3d 519). The citation means that the case is published in the *Federal Reporter*. When a case is chosen for publication, the case becomes binding precedent, sometimes called mandatory or controlling authority, in that court and in the district courts in the circuit in which the published case was heard. Attorneys may cite the case in a brief they submit to a court. The case may also have persuasive authority in other circuits and in district courts outside of the circuit with the published case. Some cases are listed with a *Federal Appendix* number (e.g., 808 F. App'x 19), an "unpublished" label, or both. Cases that appear in the *Federal Appendix* are where rulings of the US court of appeals that have not been selected for publication in the *Federal Reporter* may appear. These cases do not generate binding precedent but may be persuasive. Attorneys may also cite persuasive cases in certain circumstances.

CHAPTER 4

Researching Special Education Law Online

With the availability of online resources, today's administrators and teachers can become more legally literate about special education laws, policies, and procedures. Moreover, they should be better able to identify legal issues and applicable laws or legal standards and apply relevant legal rules to solve legal dilemmas. Because many of the legal requirements involving the education of children and youth with disabilities originated in federal statutory law, it is a good place to begin a search of special education–related legal information. Fortunately, most of these resources are readily available online.

Congress has the authority to make laws. The statutes passed or enacted by Congress are signed into law by the president. These laws are available in both print and online versions. Federal statutes can be found in the *United States Code* (USC), which is the official version of the law because it is published by the US government. All federal statutes are organized by topic as a series of volumes in the USC, which consists of fifty-four titles. All three of the leading federal statutes affecting students with disabilities—the IDEA, Section 504, and the ADA—are published in specific titles of the USC. The IDEA can be found in Title 20 (Education), Section 504 can be found in Title 29 (Labor Statutes), and the ADA can be found in Title 42 (Public Health and Welfare).

Due to significant advances in the accessibility of online legal information, many online resources provide free access to the USC that allow users to browse or search by a specific title, chapter, or section. The official website of the USC can be found on the govinfo website: https://www.govinfo.gov/app/collection/USCODE. Additionally, the USC can be accessed online through a variety of nongovernmental websites, including Cornell Law School's Legal Information Institute (LII) (https://www.law.cornell.edu/uscode/text) or FindLaw's (https://codes.findlaw.com/us/) USC online sites.

The statutes passed by Congress tend to be broad and general in nature. Therefore, Congress delegates power to the appropriate administrative agencies to create specific regulations to implement the laws. These agencies, which are part of the executive branch of government, add specifics to the general content of the law and provide procedures by which the law can be enforced. Regulations have the force of law, thus a violation of a regulation is as serious as a violation of the law.

Regulations are published in the *Code of Federal Regulations* (CFR). Like federal statutes, the CFR is available online. Two useful online resources for accessing the federal regulations relating to special education are: (a) Electronic Code of Federal Regulations (e-CFR), (https://www.ecfr.gov), which is a currently updated version of the CFR; and (b) the US Department of Education's IDEA website, which details both the statute and regulations (https://sites.ed.gov/idea/statuteregulations/#regulations). Regulations such as the CFR can be accessed online through a variety of nongovernmental websites, including Cornell Law School's Legal Information Institute (LII) (https://www.law.cornell.edu/uscode/text) or FindLaw's (https://codes.findlaw.com/us/) USC online sites.

A reference to a source of law is a citation. Legal citations are easy to read. The first number indicates the volume in which the statute or regulation is located; the next component of the citation is the abbreviation that refers to the book or series in which the material may be found (e.g., USC, CFR). The second number indicates the section of the statute, with the symbol § standing for section. For the IDEA the statute begins in 20 USC at section 1400 and ends at section 1482. The section containing the IDEA regulations is section 300. The next parts of the citation to a statute are the subsections, which locate the specific section of a law. For example, the citation for the definition of special education in the IDEA is 20 USC § 1401(29). The citation for the definition of special education in the regulations to the IDEA is 34 CFR § 300.39.

A citation to a case is also relatively easy to read. The first part of the citation is the name of the case. The name of the case is followed by the volume number and the reporter in which the case can be found (e.g., F. Supp for published district courts, F.3d for published circuit court cases, US for Supreme Court cases). The last part of a citation, which is in parenthesis, includes the name of the court and the year in which the ruling was issued. For example, the citation for *Barnett* v. *Memphis City School System*, 294 F. Supp.2d 924 (W.D. Tenn. 2003) can be found in volume 294 of the *Federal Supplement, Second Series* beginning on page 924. The case was heard at the federal district court in the Western Division of Tennessee in 2003. Cases from the US courts of appeals for the various circuits will have a citation as follows: *Spring Branch Independent School District* v. *O.W.*, 961 F.3d 781 (5th Cir. 2020). The case can be found in volume 962 of the third series of the *Federal Reporter* on page 781. The US Court of Appeals for the Fifth Circuit ruled on the case in 2020.

A citation in the official reporter for the US Supreme Court, the *Supreme Court Reporter*, will appear as *Board of Education of the Hendrick Hudson Central School District v. Rowley*, 458 U.S. 175 (1982).

Current opinions are accessible daily from official federal court websites. Every US court of appeals has a website that quickly published rulings after they are issued. The official US courts website, https://www.uscourts.gov/, provides links to the US Supreme Court and to all US courts of appeals and US district court websites. The official US Supreme Court website, https://www.supremecourt.gov/, not only publishes opinions but also includes decisions from 1991 forward, transcripts of oral arguments, and briefs. In addition, the Oyez Project website provides digital audio recordings of oral arguments before the US Supreme Court and links to the full-text versions of opinions from 1973 forward. Another excellent website is the unofficial *SCOTUS* blog (scotusblog.com).

Secondary websites include Google Scholar, FindLaw, and Justia. Many of the legal cases profiled in this book can be found on the Google Scholar website (scholar.google.com), which includes both federal and state legal opinions (see Figure 4.1). From the main Google Scholar search page, select the radio button for "case law." Type your case citation or case name in the search box and click the search button. Keyword searches of the full text of case opinions may also be conducted from this screen. Searches may be limited to federal courts and/or to particular state courts. The United States courts website provides access to the US Supreme Court, US courts of appeals, and US district court websites. Table 4.1 lists online resources for searching federal and state-level court decisions or rulings. Additionally, open-access websites, including Cornell Law School's Legal Information Institute (LII) and Google Scholar, allow users

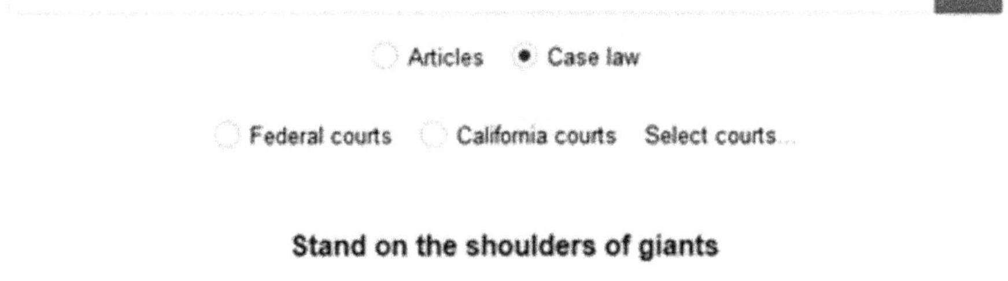

Google Scholar

○ Articles ● Case law

○ Federal courts ○ California courts ○ Select courts

Stand on the shoulders of giants

Figure 4.1 Google Scholar Website.

TABLE 4.1 Online Resources for Searching Special Education Federal and State-Level Case Law.

Name	Website
Case Law Access Project (Harvard University) (Provides access to all U.S. official published case law)	https://case.law/
Cornell Law School's Legal Information Institute (LII) (Cornell Law School) (Provides primary legal materials, legal encyclopedia, and the *Supreme Court Bulletin*)	https://www.law.cornell.edu/
Google Scholar	https://scholar.google.com
Justia	https://law.justia.com/
Oyez	http://www.oyez.org
PACER (Public Access to Court Electronic Records) (*Note*: A nominal fee is associated with accessing legal case information.)	https://www.pacer.gov/
Public Library of Law	https://www.fastcase.com/
US Supreme Court	http://supremecourt.gov
US Courts	http://uscourts.gov

to search federal and state legal cases individually or together (Yell, 2019). The Public Access to Court Electronic Records (PACER) website (https://www.pacer.gov/findcase.html) became available in 2001, allowing users to retrieve individual legal cases online from both federal appellate and district-level jurisdictions. Currently, there is a maximum charge of three dollars for online access to any single court case document other than name searches, reports that are not case-specific, and transcripts of federal court proceedings.

State laws and regulations are generally available online from the websites of their states. Individual states often organize their statutes and regulations by subject (e.g., education). Many states offer specific websites that provide access to specific state statutes and regulations. For example, Cornell Law School's Legal Information Institute (LII) allows you to search education statutes by individual state (https://www.law.cornell.edu/wex/table_education) or jurisdiction type (https://www.law.cornell.edu/states/listing).

Table 4.2 provides leading online resources through which to access special education statutes, regulations, and administrative agency policy and guidance documents. A growing number of secondary online legal resources relate to special education law and policy. One example of a secondary online resource for special education law and policy is blogs. Blogs are online discussions on a particular topic and involve informal diary-style text entries, often referred to as posts. Blogs allow law professors, higher education personnel, and education professionals to report and comment on developments in special education law as they occur. Blogs now cover everything from state-level due process hearings to cases on appeal before the US Supreme Court. Online blog posts are usually

TABLE 4.2 **Online Resources of Special Education Statutes, Regulations, and Administrative Agency Policy and Guidance Documents.**

Name	Website
50-State Survey of Special Education Laws and Regulations (Franklin County Law Library)	https://fclawlib.libguides.com/special education/50statesurvey
Americans with Disabilities Act (ADA) Homepage	https://www.ada.gov/pubs/adastatute08.htm
Cornell Law School's Legal Information Institute (CII): State Law Resources by Jurisdiction	https://www.law.cornell.edu/states/listing
e-CFR (Electronic Code of Federal Regulations)	https://www.ecfr.gov
US Department of Education, Office of Special Education Programs (OSEP) policy letters and guidance to support the implementation of the Individuals with Disabilities Education Act (IDEA)	https://sites.ed.gov/idea/policy-guidance/
US Department of Education, IDEA Statutes and Regulations	https://sites.ed.gov/idea/statuteregulations/
US Department of Labor, Section 504 of the Rehabilitation Act of 1973	https://www.dol.gov/oasam/regs/statutes/sec504.htm
US House of Representatives, Office of the Law Revision Counsel	http://uscode.house.gov

displayed in chronological order. Table 4.3 lists some of the leading special education law and policy blogs, including *SpedLawBlog* (https://spedlawblog.com), created and regularly updated by the authors of this book.

TABLE 4.3   **Online Blogs of Special Education Legal Information.**

Name	Website
Disability Scoop (Politics and Law Blog)	http://www.disabilityscoop.com/politics/
Education Law Professors Blog	https://lawprofessors.typepad.com/education_law/
SpedLawBlog	https://spedlawblog.com/
Wrightslaw Way to Special Education Law and Advocacy Blog	https://www.wrightslaw.com/blog/

CHAPTER 5

Topics Covered by US Courts of Appeals in 2020

5.1 504
Ninth Circuit
1. Esther DE LA FUENTE, on her own behalf and on behalf of A.D. v. ROOSEVELT ELEMENTARY SCHOOL DISTRICT NO. 66, a political subdivision of the State of Arizona; Jeanne N. KOBA, an individual; Jonathan MOORE, an individual: Freddy MONTOYA, an individual; Cynthia BERNACKI, an individual, and Brent RUSSELL, an individual; KELLY SERVICES, INC., a foreign corporation
2. Lexyington McINTYRE v. EUGENE SCHOOL DISTRICT 4J, and Cheryl LINDER; Andy DEY; Michael STASACK; Susie NICHOLSON; Suzie McLAUCHLIN

5.2 Abuse
Sixth Circuit
1. Jennifer GARZA, individually and as guardian ad litem for C.G. on behalf of C.G. v. LANSING SCHOOL DISTRICT; Connie NICKSON; Tracey KEATON; Martin ALWARDT; Yvonne CAAMAL CANUL; Sheryl BACON; Edna ROBINSON

Eleventh Circuit
1. Christopher GLOSTON, by Tamika GLOSTON, his next friend, parent, and natural guardian v. Jack VANCE

5.3 Administrative Remedies
Fifth Circuit
1. A.H. v. Austin Independent School District
2. Doe v. Harlandale Independent School District
3. T.B. v. Northwest Independent School District

Ninth Circuit
1. A.L., by and through her guardian, I. LEE v. CLOVIS UNIFIED SCHOOL DISTRICT et al.

2. D.D., a minor, by and through his guardian ad litem, Michaela INGRAM v. LOS ANGELES UNIFIED SCHOOL DISTRICT
3. J.F., a minor, by and through guardians ad litem Aron FEILES and Alexandra FEILES, individually on and on behalf of the proposed class v. SAN DIEGO UNIFIED SCHOOL DISTRICT, a government entity
4. K.D., a minor, by and through her guardian ad litem, Leila CARERRA v. LOS ANGELES UNIFIED SCHOOL DISTRICT
5. Lexyington McINTYRE v. EUGENE SCHOOL DISTRICT 4J, and Cheryl LINDER; Andy DEY; Michael STASACK; Susie NICHOLSON; Suzie McLAUCHLIN

5.4 Attorney's Fees
Third Circuit
1. A.B., by and through his parents and natural guardians, F.B. and N.V., of Effort, PA v. PLEASANT VALLEY SCHOOL DISTRICT
2. I.K., on behalf of Z.S. v. MONTCLAIR BOARD OF EDUCATION
3. RENA C., individually and on behalf of A.D. v. COLONIAL SCHOOL DISTRICT

Eighth Circuit
1. Chad RICHARDSON, individually, and as parents and next friends of L; Tonya RICHARDSON, individually, and as parents and next friends of L v. OMAHA SCHOOL DISTRICT; Jacob SHERWOOD, superintendent; Amanda GREEN, principal; Dawn DILLON, teacher

Ninth Circuit
1. J.M.; Marla McDONALD v. OAKLAND UNIFIED SCHOOL DISTRICT

Tenth Circuit
1. Board of Education of Gallup–McKinley County Schools v. Native American Disability Law Center

DC Circuit
1. Keith Allen et al. v. District of Columbia

5.5 Child Find
Fifth Circuit
1. P.P. v. Northwest Independent School District
2. Spring Branch Independent School District v. O.W.

5.6 Compensatory Education
Fifth Circuit
1. P.P. v. Northwest Independent School District

5.7 Discrimination
Sixth Circuit
1. Keshia CLEMONS, as mother and next friend of T.W. v. SHELBY COUNTY BOARD OF EDUCATION; Scott RICKE; John LEEPER; James NIEHOF, superintendent

Ninth Circuit

1. SAVE ACCESS ACADEMY, an unincorporated association v. MULTNOMAH COUNTY SCHOOL DISTRICT NO. 1J, an Oregon public corporate entity by and through the Board of Directors of Multnomah County School District No. 1J; Guadalupe GUERRERO, superintendent, individually and in his official capacity

5.8 Eligibility
Eighth Circuit
1. INDEPENDENT SCHOOL DISTRICT NO. 283 v. E.M.D.H., a minor, by and through her parents and next friends, L.H. and S.D., INDEPENDENT SCHOOL DISTRICT NO. 283 v. E.M.D.H., a minor, by and through her parents and next friends, L.H. and S.D.

5.9 Enrollment
Ninth Circuit
1. Regina Marie PANGERL, individually and on behalf of T.P. v. PEORIA UNIFIED SCHOOL DISTRICT

5.10 Escrow Accounts
Second Circuit
1. Jane DOE, John DOE, by and through his parent Jane DOE, plaintiffs-appellants v. EAST LYME BOARD OF EDUCATION, CONNECTICUT STATE DEPARTMENT OF EDUCATION

5.11 Evaluation
Ninth Circuit
1. BUTTE SCHOOL DISTRICT NO. 1 v. C.S.; Stuart MCCARVEL, in his capacity as originator of the C.S. due process complaint

5.12 FAPE
Third Circuit
1. K.E.; B.E., on behalf of T.E. v. NORTHERN HIGHLANDS REGIONAL BOARD OF EDUCATION

Fifth Circuit
1. A.A. & K.K. v. NORTHSIDE INDEPENDENT SCHOOL DISTRICT
2. P.P. v. Northwest Independent School District
3. R.S. v. Highland Park Independent School District
4. Spring Branch Independent School District v. O.W.

Ninth Circuit
1. BELLFLOWER UNIFIED SCHOOL DISTRICT v. Fernando LUA, individually and on behalf of minor K.L., Sandra LUA, individually and on behalf of minor K.L.
2. Terria McKNIGHT v. LYON COUNTY SCHOOL DISTRICT

Tenth Circuit
1. Donahue v. Kansas Board of Education

DC Circuit
1. Sanchez & K.B. v. District of Columbia

5.13 First Amendment
Ninth Circuit
1. L.F., in his individual capacity and as parent of K.S.F. (Student 1) and K.S.F. (Student 2); K.S.F., Student 1; K.S.F., Student 2 v. LAKE WASHINGTON SCHOOL DISTRICT #414

Fifth Circuit
1. T.B. v. Northwest Independent School District

5.14 Functional Behavior Assessment
Second Circuit
1. D.S., by and through his parents and next friends, M.S. and R.S. v. TRUMBULL BOARD OF EDUCATION

Tenth Circuit
1. Elizabeth B. v. El Paso County School District 11

5.15 Harassment
Second Circuit
1. Michele PISTELLO v. BOARD OF EDUCATION OF THE CANASTOTA CENTRAL SCHOOL DISTRICT

Sixth Circuit
1. Cherryl KIRILENKO-ISON; Susan BAUDER-SMITH v. BOARD OF EDUCATION OF DANVILLE INDEPENDENT SCHOOLS

5.16 Independent Educational Evaluation
Second Circuit
1. D.S., by and through his parents and next friends, M.S. and R.S., v. TRUMBULL BOARD OF EDUCATION

5.17 Individualized Education Program (IEP)-FAPE
Third Circuit
1. K.E.; B.E., on behalf of T.E. v. NORTHERN HIGHLANDS REGIONAL BOARD OF EDUCATION

Fifth Circuit
1. R.S. v. Highland Park Independent School District

Eighth Circuit
1. BENTONVILLE SCHOOL DISTRICT v. Lisa SMITH, as parent of M.S., a minor,

Ninth Circuit
1. Terria McKNIGHT v. LYON COUNTY SCHOOL DISTRICT

5.18 Jurisdiction
Third Circuit
1. Andrew MOYNIHAN; Karen MOYNIHAN v. WEST CHESTER AREA SCHOOL DISTRICT; PENNSYLVANIA OFFICE FOR DISPUTE RESOLUTION
2. L.W. v. JERSEY CITY BOARD OF EDUCATION; the PARSIPPANY-TROY HILLS BOARD OF EDUCATION

5.19 Least Restrictive Environment
Ninth Circuit
1. SAVE ACCESS ACADEMY, an unincorporated association v. MULTNOMAH COUNTY SCHOOL DISTRICT NO. 1J, an Oregon public corporate entity by and through the Board of Directors of Multnomah County School District No. 1J; Guadalupe GUERRERO, superintendent, individually and in his official capacity

5.20 Literacy
Sixth District
1. GARY B., JESSIE K., CRISTOPHER R., ISAIAS R., ESMERALDA V., PAUL M., and JAIME R., minors, plaintiffs v. Gretchen WHITMER et al.

5.21 Mootness
Third Circuit
1. Andrew MOYNIHAN; Karen MOYNIHAN v. WEST CHESTER AREA SCHOOL DISTRICT; PENNSYLVANIA OFFICE FOR DISPUTE RESOLUTION

Ninth Circuit
1. EVERETT H. et al. v. DRY CREEK JOINT ELEMENTARY SCHOOL DISTRICT et al.

DC Circuit
1. J.T. v. District of Columbia

5.22 Noncustodial Parents
Sixth Circuit
1. Okwuldi Francis CHUKWUANI, M.D. v. SOLON CITY SCHOOL DISTRICT

5.23 Paraprofessionals
Ninth Circuit
1. Terria McKNIGHT v. LYON COUNTY SCHOOL DISTRICT

5.24 Placement
Eighth Circuit
1. D.L., by next friend Frances LANDON, by next friend MollyJayne LANDON v. ST. LOUIS CITY SCHOOL DISTRICT

5.25 Procedural Violations
Ninth Circuit
1. BUTTE SCHOOL DISTRICT NO. 1 v. C.S.; Stuart MCCARVEL, in his capacity as originator of the C.S. due process complaint

5.26 *Pro se*
Tenth Circuit
1. Donahue v. Kansas Board of Education

5.27 Residency
Third Circuit
1. K.K.-M., individually and as kinship legal guardian of the minor children R.M. and A.W. v. NEW JERSEY DEPARTMENT OF EDUCATION; NEW JERSEY OFFICE OF ADMINISTRATIVE LAW; Dominic ROTA; GLOUCESTER CITY BOARD OF EDUCATION, doing business as Gloucester City Public Schools

5.28 Residential Placement
Ninth Circuit
1. N.G., a conserved adult, by and through her conservators, R.G. and G.G. et al. v. PLACENTIA YORBA LINDA UNIFIED SCHOOL DISTRICT

5.29 Standard for Review
Second Circuit
1. BOARD OF EDUCATION OF THE WAPPINGERS CENTRAL SCHOOL DISTRICT v. D.M., as the parent of E.M., a student with a disability, A.M., as the parent of E.M.

5.30 Statute of Limitations
Second Circuit
1. G.B., a minor, by and through his parents by next friend Nancy A. BARBOUR by next friend Cynthia L. NONEMACHER, Nancy A. BARBOUR, parent and next friend to G.B., a minor, Cynthia L. NONEMACHER, parent and next friend to G.B., a minor v. ORANGE SOUTHWEST SUPERVISORY DISTRICT

Third Circuit
1. B.B., by and through his Parents CATHERINE B. and JIMMY B. of Philadelphia Pennsylvania v. DELAWARE COLLEGE PREPARATORY ACADEMY; DELAWARE DEPARTMENT OF EDUCATION

Ninth Circuit
1. Esther DE LA FUENTE, on her own behalf and on behalf of A.D. v. ROOSEVELT ELEMENTARY SCHOOL DISTRICT NO. 66, a political subdivision of the State of Arizona; Jeanne N. KOBA, an individual; Jonathan MOORE, an individual; Freddy MONTOYA, an individual; Cynthia BERNACKI, an individual, and Brent RUSSELL, an individual; KELLY SERVICES, INC., a foreign corporation

5.31 Stay Put
Second Circuit
1. NESKE, individually and as parent and natural guardian of A.N. v. NEW YORK CITY DEPARTMENT OF EDUCATION
2. Cynthia SORIA, individually and as parent and natural guardian of G.S., Giovanni SORIA, individually and as parent and natural guardian of G.S. vs. NEW YORK CITY DEPARTMENT OF EDUCATION

3. VENTURA DE PAULINO, individually and as parent and natural guardian of R.P. v. NEW YORK CITY DEPARTMENT OF EDUCATION and NEW YORK STATE EDUCATION DEPARTMENT, Robert BRIGILIO; Maria NAVARRO CARRILLO, as parent and natural guardian of M.G. and individually; Jose GARZON, as parent and natural guardian of M.G. and individually, plaintiffs-appellees v. NEW YORK CITY DEPARTMENT OF EDUCATION

5.32 Transportation
Eighth Circuit
1. OSSEO AREA SCHOOLS, INDEPENDENT SCHOOL DISTRICT NO. 279 v. M.N.B., by and through her parent, J.B.

5.33 Tuition Reimbursement
Second Circuit
1. A.N., individually and on behalf of R.N., R.N., individually and on behalf of R.N. v. BOARD OF EDUCATION FOR THE IROQUOIS CENTRAL SCHOOL DISTRICT
2. BOARD OF EDUCATION OF THE WAPPINGERS CENTRAL SCHOOL DISTRICT v. D.M., as the parent of E.M., a student with a disability, A.M., as the parent of E.M.

Third Circuit
1. J.F. and J.F., on behalf of J.F. v. BYRAM TOWNSHIP BOARD OF EDUCATION
2. K.E.; B.E., on behalf of T.E. v. NORTHERN HIGHLANDS REGIONAL BOARD OF EDUCATION

Ninth Circuit
1. BELLFLOWER UNIFIED SCHOOL DISTRICT v. Fernando LUA, individually and on behalf of minor K.L., Sandra LUA, individually and on behalf of minor K.L.

Tenth Circuit
1. Elizabeth B. v. El Paso County School District 11

CHAPTER 6

Case Summaries by Circuit[1]

6.1 Case Summaries from the US Court of Appeals, Second Circuit — 88

    6.1.1 A.N., individually and on behalf of R.N., R.N., individually and on behalf of R.N. v. BOARD OF EDUCATION FOR THE IROQUOIS CENTRAL SCHOOL DISTRICT — 88

    6.1.2 BOARD OF EDUCATION OF THE WAPPINGERS CENTRAL SCHOOL DISTRICT v. D.M., as the parent of E.M., a student with a disability, A.M., as the parent of E.M. — 90

    6.1.3 D.S., by and through his parents and next friends, M.S. and R.S. v. TRUMBULL BOARD OF EDUCATION — 91

    6.1.4 Jane DOE, John DOE, by and through his parent Jane DOE, plaintiffs-appellants v. EAST LYME BOARD OF EDUCATION, CONNECTICUT STATE DEPARTMENT OF EDUCATION — 92

    6.1.5 G.B., a minor, by and through his parents by next friend Nancy A. BARBOUR by next friend Cynthia L. NONEMACHER, Nancy A. BARBOUR, parent and next friend to G.B., a minor, Cynthia L. NONEMACHER, parent and next friend to G.B., a minor v. ORANGE SOUTHWEST SUPERVISORY DISTRICT — 93

    6.1.6 NESKE, individually and as parent and natural guardian of A.N. v. NEW YORK CITY DEPARTMENT OF EDUCATION — 94

    6.1.7 Michele PISTELLO v. BOARD OF EDUCATION OF THE CANASTOTA CENTRAL SCHOOL DISTRICT — 95

---

1. No special education cases were found for the US Courts of Appeals for the First and Seventh Circuits.

6.1.8 Cynthia SORIA, individually and as parent and natural guardian of G.S., Giovanni SORIA, individually and as parent and natural guardian of G.S. vs. NEW YORK CITY DEPARTMENT OF EDUCATION ... 96

6.1.9 VENTURA DE PAULINO, individually and as parent and natural guardian of R.P. v. NEW YORK CITY DEPARTMENT OF EDUCATION and NEW YORK STATE EDUCATION DEPARTMENT, Robert BRIGILIO; Maria NAVARRO CARRILLO, as parent and natural guardian of M.G. and individually; Jose GARZON, as parent and natural guardian of M.G. and individually, plaintiffs-appellees v. NEW YORK CITY DEPARTMENT OF EDUCATION ... 97

6.2 Case Summaries from the US Court of Appeals, Third Circuit ... 98

6.2.1 A.B., by and through his parents and natural guardians F.B. and N.V., of Effort, PA v. PLEASANT VALLEY SCHOOL DISTRICT ... 98

6.2.2 Andrew MOYNIHAN; Karen MOYNIHAN v. WEST CHESTER AREA SCHOOL DISTRICT; PENNSYLVANIA OFFICE FOR DISPUTE RESOLUTION ... 99

6.2.3 B.B., by and through his parents CATHERINE B. and JIMMY B. of Philadelphia Pennsylvania v. DELAWARE COLLEGE PREPARATORY ACADEMY; DELAWARE DEPARTMENT OF EDUCATION ... 100

6.2.4 I.K., on behalf of Z.S. v. MONTCLAIR BOARD OF EDUCATION ... 101

6.2.5 J.F. and J.F., on behalf of J.F. v. BYRAM TOWNSHIP BOARD OF EDUCATION ... 102

6.2.6 K.E.; B.E., on behalf of T.E. v. NORTHERN HIGHLANDS REGIONAL BOARD OF EDUCATION ... 103

6.2.7 K.K.-M., individually and as kinship legal guardian of the minor children R.M. and A.W. v. NEW JERSEY DEPARTMENT OF EDUCATION; NEW JERSEY OFFICE OF ADMINISTRATIVE LAW; Dominic ROTA; GLOUCESTER CITY BOARD OF EDUCATION, doing business as Gloucester City Public Schools ... 105

6.2.8 L.W. v. JERSEY CITY BOARD OF EDUCATION; the PARSIPPANY-TROY HILLS BOARD OF EDUCATION ... 106

6.2.9 RENA C., individually and on behalf of A.D. v. COLONIAL SCHOOL DISTRICT ... 107

6.3 Case Summaries from the US Court of Appeals, Fourth Circuit ... 109

6.3.1 R.S. v. BOARD OF DIRECTORS OF WOODS CHARTER SCHOOL COMPANY ... 109

Case Summaries by Circuit **85**

6.4 Case Summaries from the US Court of Appeals, Fifth Circuit   111
- 6.4.1   A.H. v. Austin Independent School District   111
- 6.4.2   A.A. & K.K. v. NORTHSIDE INDEPENDENT SCHOOL DISTRICT   113
- 6.4.3   Doe v. Harlandale Independent School District   115
- 6.4.4   P.P. v. Northwest Independent School District   116
- 6.4.5   R.S. v. Highland Park Independent School District   118
- 6.4.6   Spring Branch Independent School District v. O.W.   121
- 6.4.7   T.B. v. Northwest Independent School District   123

6.5 Case Summaries of the US Court of Appeals, Sixth Circuit   126
- 6.5.1   Okwuldi Francis CHUKWUANI, M.D. v. SOLON CITY SCHOOL DISTRICT   126
- 6.5.2   Keshia CLEMONS, as mother and next friend of T.W. v. SHELBY COUNTY BOARD OF EDUCATION; Scott RICKE; John LEEPER; James NIEHOF, superintendent   127
- 6.5.3   GARY B., JESSIE K., CRISTOPHER R., ISAIAS R., ESMERALDA V., PAUL M., and JAIME R., minors, plaintiffs v. Gretchen WHITMER et al.   129
- 6.5.4   Jennifer GARZA, individually and as guardian ad litem for C.G. on behalf of C.G. v. LANSING SCHOOL DISTRICT; Connie NICKSON; Tracey KEATON; Martin ALWARDT; Yvonne CAAMAL CANUL; Sheryl BACON; Edna ROBINSON   130
- 6.5.5   Cherryl KIRILENKO-ISON; Susan BAUDER-SMITH v. BOARD OF EDUCATION OF DANVILLE INDEPENDENT SCHOOLS   132

6.6 Case Summaries from the US Court of Appeals, Eighth Circuit   133
- 6.6.1   BENTONVILLE SCHOOL DISTRICT v. Lisa SMITH, as parent of M.S., a minor   133
- 6.6.2   D.L., by next friend Frances LANDON, by next friend MollyJayne LANDON v. ST. LOUIS CITY SCHOOL DISTRICT   134
- 6.6.3   INDEPENDENT SCHOOL DISTRICT NO. 283 v. E.M.D.H., a minor, by and through her parents and next friends, L.H. and S.D.   135
- 6.6.4   OSSEO AREA SCHOOLS, INDEPENDENT SCHOOL DISTRICT NO. 279 v. M.N.B., by and through her parent, J.B.   136
- 6.6.5   Chad RICHARDSON, individually, and as parent and next friend of L; Tonya RICHARDSON, individually, and as parent and next friend of L v. OMAHA SCHOOL DISTRICT; Jacob SHERWOOD, superintendent; Amanda GREEN, principal; Dawn DILLON, teacher   137

86 Chapter 6

6.7 Case Summaries from the US Court of Appeals, Ninth Circuit   138

    6.7.1   A.L., by and through her guardian, I. LEE v. CLOVIS UNIFIED SCHOOL DISTRICT et al.   138

    6.7.2   BELLFLOWER UNIFIED SCHOOL DISTRICT v. Fernando LUA, individually and on behalf of minor K.L., Sandra LUA, individually and on behalf of minor K.L.   139

    6.7.3   BUTTE SCHOOL DISTRICT NO. 1 v. C.S.; Stuart MCCARVEL, in his capacity as originator of the C.S. due process complaint   140

    6.7.4   D.D., a minor, by and through his guardian ad litem, Michaela INGRAM v. LOS ANGELES UNIFIED SCHOOL DISTRICT   142

    6.7.5   Esther DE LA FUENTE, on her own behalf and on behalf of A.D. v. ROOSEVELT ELEMENTARY SCHOOL DISTRICT NO. 66, a political subdivision of the State of Arizona; Jeanne N. KOBA, an individual; Jonathan MOORE, an individual; Freddy MONTOYA, an individual; Cynthia BERNACKI, an individual, and Brent RUSSELL, an individual; KELLY SERVICES, INC., a foreign corporation   144

    6.7.6   EVERETT H. et al. v. DRY CREEK JOINT ELEMENTARY SCHOOL DISTRICT et al.   145

    6.7.8   J.F., a minor, by and through guardians ad litem Aron FEILES and Alexandra FEILES, individually on and on behalf of the proposed class v. SAN DIEGO UNIFIED SCHOOL DISTRICT, a government entity   146

    6.7.9   J.M.; Marla McDONALD v. OAKLAND UNIFIED SCHOOL DISTRICT   147

    6.7.10   K.D., a minor, by and through her guardian ad litem Leila CARERRA v. LOS ANGELES UNIFIED SCHOOL DISTRICT   148

    6.7.11   L.F., in his individual capacity and as parent of K.S.F (Student 1) and K.S.F. (Student 2); K.S.F., Student 1; K.S.F., Student 2 v. LAKE WASHINGTON SCHOOL DISTRICT #414   150

    6.7.12   Lexyington McINTYRE v. EUGENE SCHOOL DISTRICT 4J, and Cheryl LINDER; Andy DEY; Michael STASACK; Susie NICHOLSON; Suzie McLAUCHLIN   151

    6.7.13   Terria McKNIGHT v. LYON COUNTY SCHOOL DISTRICT   153

    6.7.14   N.G., a conserved adult, by and through her conservators R.G. and G.G. et al. v. PLACENTIA YORBA LINDA UNIFIED SCHOOL DISTRICT   154

Case Summaries by Circuit **87**

    6.7.15 Regina Marie PANGERL, individually and on behalf of T.P. v. PEORIA UNIFIED SCHOOL DISTRICT   156

    6.7.16 SAVE ACCESS ACADEMY, an unincorporated association v. MULTNOMAH COUNTY SCHOOL DISTRICT NO. 1J, an Oregon public corporate entity by and through the Board of Directors of Multnomah County School District No. 1J; Guadalupe GUERRERO, superintendent, individually and in his official capacity   157

6.8 Case Summaries from the US Court of Appeals, Tenth Circuit   158

    6.8.1 Donahue v. Kansas Board of Education   158

    6.8.2 Elizabeth B. v. El Paso County School District 11   160

    6.8.3 Board of Education of Gallup-McKinley County Schools v. Native American Disability Law Center   162

6.9 Case Summaries from the US Court of Appeals, Eleventh Circuit   163

    6.9.1 Christopher GLOSTON, by Tamika GLOSTON, his next friend, parent, and natural guardian v. Jack VANCE   163

6.10 Case Summaries from the US Court of Appeals, DC Circuit   164

    6.10.1 Sanchez & Z.B. v. DISTRICT OF COLUMBIA PUBLIC SCHOOLS   164

    6.10.2 Keith Allen et al. v. DISTRICT OF COLUMBIA   166

    6.10.3 J.T. v. DISTRICT OF COLUMBIA   168

6.1 Case Summaries from the US Court of Appeals, Second Circuit

6.1.1

A.N., individually and on behalf of R.N., R.N., individually and on behalf of R.N. v. BOARD OF EDUCATION FOR THE IROQUOIS CENTRAL SCHOOL DISTRICT

801 F. App'x 35

US Court of Appeals, Second Circuit

April 14, 2020

-Unpublished-

Issue:

- Legal standard of review under the IDEA for tuition reimbursement paid to a private school.

Facts of the case:

In this case the parents of a seventh grade student with dyslexia sought tuition reimbursement paid to a private school based on their son's enrollment from the period of February 1, 2013, through June 30, 2013. The parents maintained the school district denied their son a FAPE as required under the IDEA. Specifically, the parents argued in this case that their son's IEP was inadequate to provide meaningful educational advancement. On appeal the school district contended the district court erred in rejecting the analysis of the SRO, who concluded that the parents were not legally entitled to tuition reimbursement because the school district had provided a successful FAPE to the student.

Ruling:

The US Circuit Court of Appeals for the Second Circuit upheld a previous district court's tuition reimbursement award to R.N.'s parents. The appellate court found the district court's prior decision well supported and persuasive since the SRO's conclusions were unpersuasive and did not apply the correct legal test for tuition reimbursement.

Significance to educators:

Under what is referred to as the "*Burlington-Carter* test" parents of IDEA–eligible students who have unilaterally placed or enrolled their child in a private school are legally entitled to reimbursement (retroactively) if the following three conditions are satisfied: (1) the school district's proposed placement violated the IDEA, (2) the parents' alternative private placement is appropriate to meet the child's needs, and (3) equitable considerations favor reimbursement. See *Florence Community School District Four* v. *Carter ex rel. Carter*, 510 U.S. 7 (1993) and *School Community of Town of Burlington, Massachusetts* v. *Department of Education of Massachusetts*, 471 U.S. 369 (1985).

6.1.2

BOARD OF EDUCATION OF THE WAPPINGERS CENTRAL SCHOOL DISTRICT v. D.M., *as the parent of E.M., a student with a disability,* A.M., *as the parent of E.M.*

US Court of Appeals, Second Circuit

December 18, 2020

Issues:

- Legal standard of review for an SRO's decision.
- Tuition reimbursement for unilateral placement in a private school under the IDEA.

Facts of the case:

A New York public school district appealed a prior judgment by a New York district court in favor of the parents of a student with autism. The district court's ruling affirmed a decision by a New York State Education Department SRO requiring the school district to reimburse the student's tuition at a private school for the 2017–2018 school year.

Ruling:

The appellate court upheld an earlier SRO determination that the parents of a student with autism were legally entitled to tuition reimbursement for their unilateral private school placement because a New York school district's proposed IEP was insufficient to provide the student with a FAPE under the IDEA. In their legal decision, the appellate court maintained the SRO had "thoroughly and carefully" reviewed the record when making his or her decision, declined to interfere with the SRO's "well-reasoned" ruling, and affirmed judgment for the parents. Because there was no evidence the SRO's findings were unsupported, the Second Circuit ruled there was no reason to overturn the SRO's findings that the student E.M.'s placement in a private school was appropriate and the student's parents were legally entitled to tuition reimbursement for the entire 2017–2018 school year.

Significance to educators:

Unless an IHO or SRO's findings are unsupported by evidence, courts must accept the factual findings of the IHO or SRO. Therefore, any court (at any level) generally cannot overturn an IHO or SRO decision simply because the court would have reached a different conclusion.

6.1.3

D.S., by and through his parents and next friends, M.S. and R.S. v.
TRUMBULL BOARD OF EDUCATION

US Court of Appeals, Second Circuit

September 17, 2020

Issues:

- Functional behavioral assessments.
- Independent educational evaluations.

Facts of the case:

The parents of an eighth-grade student diagnosed with ADHD as well as other developmental and behavioral disorders sought review of a decision made by an IHO granting the request under the IDEA for an IEE at public expense for both a psychosocial and behavior assessment but denying the request for multiple additional assessments at public expense during the student's triennial evaluation. The parents also disagreed with the Connecticut school district's FBA.

Ruling:

The appellate court ruled in favor of the school district because an FBA is not officially an "evaluation" that gives parents the legal right to a publicly funded IEE. This ruling represents a departure from a long-standing view that any parent who disagrees with their child's FBA has a right to an IEE at public expense. Instead, the appellate court held the IDEA discusses FBAs as evaluations only in the context of publicly funded IEEs and does not address issues related to parental consent or a parent's ability to legally challenge their child's FBA as a valid assessment tool.

Significance to educators:

It has usually been a long-standing perspective reinforced by legal precedence that parents who disagree with their child's FBA have the legal right to an IEE at public expense. Based on this recent case, however, school districts in the states of Connecticut, New York, and Vermont need to consider potential challenges to this viewpoint when responding to formal requests for publicly funded IEEs that allege inappropriate FBAs, especially those that question the validity of FBAs as assessment tools.

6.1.4

***Jane DOE, John DOE, by and through his parent Jane DOE, plaintiffs-appellants* v. EAST LYME BOARD OF EDUCATION, CONNECTICUT STATE DEPARTMENT OF EDUCATION**

962 F.3d 649

US Court of Appeals, Second Circuit

June 18, 2020

Issue:

- Trust funds and escrow accounts under the IDEA.

Facts of the case:

The parent of a student with autism brought legal action against a Connecticut school district under the IDEA, alleging the school district failed to provide her child with a FAPE by refusing to pay for services mandated by the student's IEP. A previous district court decision awarded the parent reimbursement for her out-of-pocket expenses related to services covered by the student's stay-put IEP but denied reimbursement for tuition and services not mandated by the IEP. The district court also ordered compensatory funds to be placed into an escrow account with certain restrictions. The parent appealed and argued that she should be reimbursed for all tuition payments as well as other expenses and that the award structure was currently inequitable.

Ruling:

The appellate court partially vacated the decision and remanded the case for further proceedings with instructions to remove both provisions from the student's compensatory education award. While the Second Circuit ruled limitations on the escrow account were permissible, an escrow agent's power to unilaterally reduce the parent's access to the compensatory award violated the IDEA's requirement that adjustments to an award be justified to an IHO. Specifically, the appellate court agreed with the parent that the district court erred in ordering her to pay 50 percent of the maintenance fees for the escrow account.

Significance to educators:

Both courts and IHOs cannot delegate their legal authority to determine a student's compensatory education award and whether to compensate the student for a denial of FAPE or a stay-put violation.

6.1.5

G.B., a minor, by and through his parents by next friend Nancy A. BARBOUR by next friend Cynthia L. NONEMACHER, Nancy A. BARBOUR, parent and next friend to G.B., a minor, Cynthia L. NONEMACHER, parent and next friend to G.B., a minor v. ORANGE SOUTHWEST SUPERVISORY DISTRICT

US Court of Appeals, Second Circuit

December 8, 2020

-Unpublished-

Issue:

- Timeliness of statute of limitations under the IDEA.

Facts of the case:

The parents of a student with a disability made three arguments on appeal in this case. First, the IHO and the school district court erred in finding certain legal claims were time barred or the statute of limitations ran out. Second, the school district legally complied with its child-find duties. Third, the parents in this case failed to exhaust their administrative remedies as required under certain claims of the IDEA. The parents in this case did not dispute that their child-find legal claim related to the school district's failure to timely evaluate their son is subject to a two-year statute of limitations and that their claim for tuition reimbursement is subject to a ninety-day statute of limitations. Instead, the parents argued the IDEA's two-year statute of limitations should not have been allowed because they were not provided with the mandatory notices set forth under IDEA until September 2017 and the school district's preplacement evaluation was ongoing until December 2017, meaning the statute of limitations would not start to run until September 2017 at the earliest and their April 2018 due process complaint was timely.

Ruling:

The court of appeals held in favor of the school district based on the parents' own delay in filing a child-find complaint. Since school districts are legally entitled to fair notice of a FAPE claim brought against them, the circuit court found no reason to discontinue or pause the IDEA's two-year statute of limitations.

Significance to educators:

A school district may be able to successfully address efforts to pause the IDEA's two-year statute of limitations by showing parents or legal guardians of an IDEA–eligible student did not mention any withholding of information by the school district in their due process complaint. Relatedly, parents bringing these particular legal claims must exhaust all of their administrative remedies before taking their legal claims to court.

6.1.6

NESKE, individually and as parent and natural guardian of A.N. v. NEW YORK CITY DEPARTMENT OF EDUCATION

US Court of Appeals, Second Circuit

October 2, 2020

-Unpublished-

Issue:

- Stay-put provision of the IDEA.

Facts of the case:

This lawsuit challenged the New York City Department of Education's refusal to provide tuition reimbursement for an eight-year-old boy's unilateral placement in a private school for children with traumatic brain injuries. The school district argued its stay-put legal obligation ended when the parents withdrew the child from another private school for children with traumatic brain injuries.

Ruling:

The US Court of Appeals for the Second Circuit upheld a prior New York district court's ruling that dismissed the parents' pendency claim. The appellate court reasoned the school district's funding of the child's placement in the first private school for students with traumatic brain injuries undercut the parents' legal claim that the first private school was no longer available.

Significance to educators:

Under the IDEA parents of students with disabilities cannot unilaterally change their child's stay-put placements. As in this case, parents who are dissatisfied with their child's stay-put placement cannot order the school district to find another private school program of their choosing.

6.1.7

Michele PISTELLO v. BOARD OF EDUCATION OF THE CANASTOTA CENTRAL SCHOOL DISTRICT

US Court of Appeals, Second Circuit

808 F. App'x 19

April 10, 2020

Issue:

- Harassment/retaliation against special education teachers/instructors.

Facts of the case:

Michele Pistello, a special education teacher for the Canastona Central School District, accused the school district in an email of failing to comply with the IEPs of select students with disabilities. Several months after sending the email, Ms. Pistello filed a harassment report against the school district claiming retaliation following her email under both the ADA and Title VII of the Civil Rights Act of 1964. In a period of approximately six months, Ms. Pistello had also received numerous official reprimands from the school. The school district dropped all these reprimands once Ms. Pistello retained legal counsel.

Ruling:

The US Court of Appeals for the Second Circuit held the special education teacher (Ms. Pistello) presented enough evidence to warrant a jury trial of her legal claim that her former New York school district employer retaliated against her based on her filing of a harassment complaint and notifying her supervisors of potential violation of and noncompliance with the IDEA. As a result the appellate court remanded the special education teacher's retaliation claims for a jury trial.

Significance to educators:

According to the appellate court's decision in this case, school districts must be prepared to defend their decision to take formal disciplinary action against an employee so the district's actions do not appear retaliatory, especially when the employer's disciplinary actions appear close in time to the teacher's harassment complaint. In this case the school district reprimanded the teacher numerous times soon after she had filed a formal harassment complaint against the school district. In its ruling the Second Circuit explained that to successfully state a retaliation claim, the special education teacher needed to show three factors: (1) the teacher engaged in a protected activity, (2) the teacher suffered an adverse action, and (3) there was a causal connection between the protected activity and the adverse action.

6.1.8

Cynthia SORIA, individually and as parent and natural guardian of G.S., Giovanni SORIA, individually and as parent and natural guardian of G.S. v. NEW YORK CITY DEPARTMENT OF EDUCATION

US Court of Appeals, Second Circuit

October 28, 2020

-Unpublished-

Issue:

- Stay-put provision of the IDEA.

Facts of the case:

The parents of a child with a disability filed a legal complaint against the New York City Department of Education seeking an order vacating an SRO decision affirming denial of their request for public funding of their child's tuition at a new private school during pendency of the IEP challenge and pursuant to the stay-put provision of the IDEA.

Ruling:

The US Court of Appeals for the Second Circuit held the parents were not legally entitled to public funding of their child's tuition at the new private school after unilaterally transferring the child to that school. The appellate court reasoned the student's removal from the first private school designated as his stay-put placement relieved the school district of its tuition reimbursement obligations.

Significance to educators:

The IDEA does not legally require school districts to fund a private school placement while the parents' DPH is ongoing. When parents unilaterally move their child from their first pendency placement to a new private school placement, the public school district is no longer legally responsible to pay for another private school of the parents' choosing.

6.1.9

VENTURA DE PAULINO, individually and as parent and natural guardian of R.P. v. NEW YORK CITY DEPARTMENT OF EDUCATION and NEW YORK STATE EDUCATION DEPARTMENT, Robert BRIGILIO; Maria NAVARRO CARRILLO, as parent and natural guardian of M.G. and individually; Jose GARZON, as parent and natural guardian of M.G. and individually, plaintiffs-appellees v. NEW YORK CITY DEPARTMENT OF EDUCATION

959 F.3d 519

US Court of Appeals, Second Circuit

May 18, 2020

Issue:

- Stay-put provision of the IDEA.

Facts of the case:

The parents of two unrelated students with traumatic brain injuries chose to withdraw their children from one private school and enroll them into a second private school. Both parents filed legal suits against the New York City Department of Education under the IDEA seeking public funding for the new private schools' tuition and services during the pendency of the students' ongoing IEP disputes. The two parents had transferred their children from one private school to another based on their dissatisfaction with recent changes in the initial private school's management.

Ruling:

The US Court of Appeals for the Second Circuit held the school district, rather than the parents, had the authority to decide how the students' agreed-upon educational program was to be provided until the IEP dispute was resolved.

Significance to educators:

The IDEA's stay-put provision provides that, while administrative and judicial proceedings are pending and unless a school district and parents agree otherwise, a child must remain at public expense in their current educational placement. Parents who are dissatisfied with their child's education can, under the IDEA, unilaterally change their child's placement during the pendency of review proceedings and can pay for private services, including private school tuition, but are doing so at their own financial risk.

6.2 Case Summaries from the US Court of Appeals, Third Circuit

6.2.1

A.B., by and through his parents and natural guardians, F.B. and N.V., of Effort, PA v. PLEASANT VALLEY SCHOOL DISTRICT

US Court of Appeals, Third Circuit

December 3, 2020

Issue:

- Reasonableness of an attorney's fees.

Facts of the case:

In this unpublished case a Pennsylvania school district challenged parents' failure to provide objective evidence of the hourly rates for attorney's fees typically charged in the community and as a result significantly reduces its liability in an IDEA case. As a part of their case the parents stated very few attorneys represent parents in special education matters in their part of Pennsylvania. Narrowing the range to the prevailing community rate was therefore inappropriate. The decision noted the parents' submissions of prevailing fees refuted their argument in that in other parts of the state attorneys representing parents in special education matters were typically charging $375 an hour.

Ruling:

The parent's attorney was not entitled to $525 an hour, but instead was awarded $300 and $375 an hour for work on the case and the parents bore the burden of proving their fee request was reasonable. The Third Circuit also upheld the district court's reduction of the overall fee award from $118,180 to $64,999 in order to reflect the parents' incomplete success at the administrative level. The Third Circuit held the reduced fee rate was appropriate.

Significance to educators:

Reimbursement for attorney fees is determined by looking to the rates prevailing in the community for similar services by lawyers of reasonably comparable skill, experience, and reputation.

6.2.2

Andrew MOYNIHAN; Karen MOYNIHAN v. WEST CHESTER AREA SCHOOL DISTRICT; PENNSYLVANIA OFFICE FOR DISPUTE RESOLUTION

US Court of Appeals, Third Circuit

August 3, 2020

Issues:

- Whether the court has jurisdiction over the matter.
- Whether the topic is moot.

Facts of the case:

The parents of a student with Asperger syndrome and social anxiety disorder claimed the district failed to provide an appropriate education during the student's ninth, tenth, and eleventh grade school years. A DPH officer denied their claims. The parents appealed to the district court seeking, among other relief, "reimbursement for … out-of-pocket expenses" incurred in the school years when their son was allegedly denied a FAPE. The district court dismissed the remaining claims against the district *sua sponte* for lack of subject matter jurisdiction, finding the parents had requested only injunctive relief and such claims for relief were mooted by their son's graduation. The parents appealed.

Ruling:

When a student challenges a school policy, "graduation typically moots her claim for injunctive or declaratory relief." However, the parents were also seeking claims for reimbursement. This claim was not moot and therefore was remanded to the district court.

Significance to educators:

After graduation students may still sue for the cost of the services that should have been provided as required under the FAPE provision of the IDEA. The parents may also sue for compensatory education in order to make up for what should have been provided prior to graduation. A student's graduation does not prevent litigation.

6.2.3

B.B., by and through his parents CATHERINE B. and JIMMY B. of Philadelphia Pennsylvania v. DELAWARE COLLEGE PREPARATORY ACADEMY; DELAWARE DEPARTMENT OF EDUCATION

803 F. App'x 593

US Court of Appeals, Third Circuit

February 11, 2020

-Unpublished-

Issue:

- Statute of limitations for filing a DPH.

Facts of the case:

In February 2014 parents filed a DPH request involving their kindergartner, who was eligible for speech and language services. The parents withdrew their DPH request in May 2014. In April 2016 the parents filed another DPH request for denial of FAPE that occurred between May and September 2014. The parents knew about possible IDEA violations in 2014, as evidenced by their filing a previous DPH request. Even though the claims were similar, the parents could still address any issue that had occurred in the two years prior to the DPH request. The parents alleged the school violated the IDEA between May and September 2014 by failing to reevaluate their son, implement his IEP, or provide necessary transportation services.

Ruling:

Parents have two years from the date they knew or should have known about possible violations to file a claim. Because the events in question occurred within two years of the April 2016 filing, they could seek adjudication on those issues.

Significance to educators:

Even after a parent withdraws a DPH request, a school district should be able to defend itself for the services provided for the past two years. The two-year statute of limitations applies.

6.2.4

I.K., on behalf of Z.S. v. MONTCLAIR BOARD OF EDUCATION
US Court of Appeals, Third Circuit
July 16, 2020
-Unpublished-

Issue:

- Both parties requested attorney's fees.

Facts of the case:

A district proposed an IEP for an eligible student and the child's parent disagreed with the plan. That disagreement prompted the parent to request several independent evaluations of the child. The parent also sought to mediate the dispute and reached an agreement with the district to place the child in a full-day inclusion classroom. The parties could not resolve the second component of their dispute—the request for independent evaluations—and the parent petitioned for relief with the New Jersey Office of Administrative Law. An ALJ rejected that petition without holding a hearing.

Afterward the parent filed a six-count complaint against the district in federal court. The first five counts alleged statutory violations of federal and New Jersey law; the sixth count appealed the rejection of her petition for independent evaluations and requested a remand for a hearing. In moving for summary judgment on those claims, the parent urged the district court to rule on the five statutory claims and to refrain from remanding the case for a hearing. In exercising jurisdiction over the dispute, the district court partially granted summary judgment on the sixth count and remanded the case for a hearing. As for the five statutory counts, the district court retained jurisdiction over them and stayed them pending the outcome of the remanded administrative hearing.

Following that order the parent moved for attorney's fees under the IDEA. She asserted that because she received the relief originally requested—a remand for a hearing—she was a prevailing party. In awarding her fees on that basis, the district court discounted her requested fees by 50 percent across the board. That split left neither party content, so both appeal. The parent disputed the reduction, and the district argued the parent did not meet the burden of proving the reasonableness of the fees, was not a prevailing party, and certain fee requests were not compensable.

Ruling:

Since the district court left other claims pending and retained jurisdiction over this dispute during the remand, the fee award does not constitute an appealable order—leaving the Third Circuit Court without appellate jurisdiction.

Significance to educators:

Parents can sue for attorney's fees when the case is complete and they are the prevailing party.

6.2.5

J.F. and J.F., on behalf of J.F. v. BYRAM TOWNSHIP BOARD OF EDUCATION

812 F. App'x 79

US Court of Appeals, Third Circuit

May 14, 2020

-Unpublished-

Issue:

- Equitable considerations for private school tuition reimbursement.

Facts of the case:

In a public school district a student and his parents entered into an agreement and created an IEP where the student would attend a private school. At the end of the year the parents moved to a new district and sought a meeting with the new district to discuss their son's education plan for the next school year. The parents also provided the new district with their son's IEP. The parents met with the district representatives and the district informed the parents it would adopt the previous district's IEP and implement it through in-district programming, instead of at the private school. The parents did not agree with this plan, as they wanted their son to continue at the private school. The parents did not visit the school district placement. Instead, they placed their son at the private school without informing the district their son would not attend the in-district school and they would seek reimbursement for their expenses. The district informed the parents they would not be reimbursed for the private school because the parents had not provided proper notice and the district was able to provide a comparable educational program. The parents maintained they were seeking reimbursement. The district reiterated it would not reimburse the parents but again invited the parents to bring their son for a visit.

Ruling:

The parents were not entitled to reimbursement for the private school. The parents failed to give proper written notice to the district that they intended to enroll their son at the private school. The parents placed their son at the private school before they even attended a meeting with the district. The parents were required to provide written notice "[a]t least 10 business days" before placing their son at the private school. They did not do so.

Significance to educators:

Districts should work closely with parents to implement transfer IEPs in a timely fashion. Additionally, districts should keep track of all meetings, attempts to meet, and information provided to parents when a student moves to the district. Finally, districts should invite parents to visit schools/classrooms so they can visualize the possible location(s) of programming for the student.

6.2.6

K.E.; B.E., on behalf of T.E. v. NORTHERN HIGHLANDS REGIONAL BOARD OF EDUCATION

US Court of Appeals, Third Circuit

December 16, 2020

-Unpublished-

Issues:

- Equitable considerations for tuition reimbursement.
- Determination of FAPE.
- Appropriateness of a student's IEP.

Facts of the case:

A high school student who was previously eligible only for speech-language services was repeatedly bullied after a surgery in eighth grade. Over time the student was diagnosed with anxiety and depression. The district provided him with a one-on-one aide, but that did not prevent the student from being tackled on a field day. The parents were concerned about their son's safety and approached the district. The district offered a Section 504 plan that provided for the student to leave class five minutes early so as not to encounter the bullying students in the halls.

The parents rejected the Section 504 plan and sought additional accommodations. The parents unsuccessfully tried to meet with the principal prior to the start of the new school year. The parents enrolled their son in private school. At the start of the school year, there was no offer of an IEP or any changes to the Section 504 plan. The parents were also seeking a neuropsychological exam, and the district said it would not meet with the parents until the exam was complete. The report found the student suffered from anxiety and depression and included diagnoses of traumatic brain injury, seizure activity, ADHD, learning disorder, and coordination disorder. The top-line accommodations were that the student was educated in "a smaller and structured school environment" and he worked "with a learning specialist individually" on a regular basis. The new IEP did not reference the report and included the Section 504 recommendation the parents previously rejected. The parents filed a DPH request seeking tuition reimbursement. The ALJ stated, without supporting evidence, that the district was providing a FAPE and that the parents had placed the student in the private placement prior to notifying the district; therefore they were not due tuition reimbursement.

Ruling:

The parents could seek a new determination about whether they are warranted reimbursement for their son's unilateral placement at a private school. The case was remanded to the district court.

Significance to educators:

Take all claims of bullying seriously. Parents need to provide notice; however, not providing notice may not prevent a tuition reimbursement claim. Strongly consider all recommendations from independent reports and provide supports when necessary for students based on those recommendations.

6.2.7

K.K.-M., individually and as kinship legal guardian of the minor children R.M. and A.W. v. *NEW JERSEY DEPARTMENT OF EDUCATION; NEW JERSEY OFFICE OF ADMINISTRATIVE LAW; Dominic ROTA; GLOUCESTER CITY BOARD OF EDUCATION, doing business as Gloucester City Public Schools*

801 F. App'x 848

US Court of Appeals, Third Circuit

April 23, 2020

-Unpublished-

Issue:

- Students continuing to receive services from a district in which they no longer reside.

Facts of the case:

A New Jersey district terminated two siblings' enrollments based on residency. Their guardian argued the IDEA and other federal statutes allowed her two children to remain in a public school district where they no longer lived. The district court concluded the guardian did not have standing to bring her case when the complaint was initially filed and therefore held it did not have subject matter jurisdiction over the case. The district court dismissed the case with prejudice. The guardian alleged factual developments since the commencement of the litigation that were potentially relevant to a new standing inquiry.

Ruling:

The guardian of two siblings with disabilities does not have grounds for challenging a New Jersey district's residency determination. However, a permanent dismissal of a temporary restraining order was an error. The appellate court vacated the district court's dismissal order with instructions to dismiss the case without prejudice.

Significance to educators:

District officials should keep close track of files ensuring students who are residents receive an appropriate education. Also, districts should keep records of student services for previous years.

6.2.8

L.W. v. JERSEY CITY BOARD OF EDUCATION; the PARSIPPANY-TROY HILLS BOARD OF EDUCATION

US Court of Appeals, Third Circuit

August 19, 2020

-Unpublished-

Issue:

- Courts' jurisdiction over special education matters involving adults.

Facts of the case:

A former student, now a twenty-six-year-old adult, had attended the school district from 1999 to 2010. Though an evaluation found the student needed special educational assistance, the district could not obtain consent from the parents. As a result, the student received no special education. Well after graduation the former student filed a DPH request. Without holding a hearing, the ALJ ruled the claims were time-barred. The student appealed the ALJ's decision, and the parties both moved for summary judgment. The district court denied both motions, finding unresolved factual issues from gaps in the record. The district court held because the ALJ had not held a DPH, the record "fail[ed] to answer basic and preliminary questions regarding what the student's parents knew at any given point in time." As a result the district court remanded the case to the ALJ with instructions to hold a DPH and address the open issues. The former student then appealed the remand to the US Court of Appeals for the Third Circuit.

Ruling:

Determining it could only consider final decisions, the US Court of Appeals for the Third Circuit dismissed the student's appeal of the remand order.

Significance to educators:

There may be requests for back services well after a student graduates or has aged out of a program. Keep all records.

6.2.9

RENA C., individually and on behalf of A.D. v. COLONIAL SCHOOL DISTRICT

US Court of Appeals, Third Circuit

December 16, 2020

-Unpublished-

Issue:

- Rejection of a settlement offer and payment of attorney's fees.

Facts of the case:

As a result of a 2018 case out of the Third Circuit, an eligible child was enrolled in a private school because the district "had failed to provide a free, appropriate public education" *Rena C. v. Colonial Sch. Dist.*, 890 F.3d 404, 411 (3d Cir. 2018). The district was ordered to reimburse the parent's private school tuition "until Colonial convened an appropriate IEP meeting." The district offered an IEP to return the student to the district. The parent disputed the IEP's adequacy and notified the district she intended to enroll the student in private school again for the following school year, "request[ing] reimbursement for tuition and related expenses." The district claimed the new IEP was adequate and it therefore had no obligation to reimburse any educational expenses. The parent filed an administrative complaint challenging the adequacy of the IEP and seeking "declaratory relief and reimbursement for private tuition and associated costs ('tuition reimbursement') arising from the student's private placements" for the relevant school years. Prior to the administrative hearing on that complaint, the district provided the parent with a written offer to pay for the student's private school tuition and transportation. The parent rejected the offer, claiming it was not valid and was "inadequate for failing to address attorney's fees or pendency." "The parties attempted negotiation, but eventually proceeded to an administrative hearing," engaged in mediation, and ultimately "stipulated to a consent order entered by an administrative hearing office providing for tuition, one-on-one instruction support, transportation, and pendency at" a private school.

As the prevailing party, the parent filed a claim for reasonable attorney's fees. The district court granted summary judgment on her claim, agreeing she was eligible to recover attorney's fees as the prevailing party. But, pursuant to the IDEA's fee provisions, the court imposed a temporal limitation, permitting her recovery only for the fees she accrued before the district had extended its written settlement offer. The court determined the relief the parent finally obtained was not more favorable to her than the district's offer of settlement. The district court awarded her attorney's fees only for work performed to the date the ten-day offer expired.

In a previous submission to the Third Circuit, the court had concluded she was justified since the offer didn't include attorney's fees that the district should have reasonably believed would have accrued. It reversed and remanded.

On remand the district court divided the attorney hours in half because time wasn't allocated on an issue-by-issue basis and based upon the extent of the parent's success. She appealed again.

Ruling:

The US Circuit Court of Appeals for the Third Circuit found for the parent and remanded the case to the district court in order to recalculate the prevailing status on the whole case, not issue by issue.

Significance to educators:

Pay close attention to the district's ten-day letter of offer of settlement. Ensure settlement offers address attorney's fees.

6.3 Case Summaries from the US Court of Appeals, Fourth Circuit

6.3.1

R.S. v. BOARD OF DIRECTORS OF WOODS CHARTER SCHOOL COMPANY

US Court of Appeals, Fourth Circuit

May 27, 2020

-Unpublished-

Issues:

- Remedies for violations of the IDEA.
- Calculation of awards for IDEA violations.

Facts of the case:

R.S. was a student who transferred to a charter school in the Wake County Public School System of North Carolina. He had an IEP in which he received adapted physical education. However, the new charter school only provided physical education with some modifications rather than the adapted physical education program called for in R.S.'s IEP. R.S's parents initiated a DPH against the school district, the board of the charter school, and the North Carolina Department of Education. An ALJ found the charter school had denied R.S. a FAPE and awarded him extensive compensatory educational services. An appeal to an SRO overturned many of the ALJ's conclusions of law and lowered the number of compensatory services awarded. R.S. filed a civil action in the US District Court of North Carolina.

The district court judge noted the Fourth Circuit Court had previously cautioned district courts against rejecting an IHO's findings of fact because of disagreements about credibility determinations or the IHO's seeming failure to explain his or her findings in sufficient detail. Similarly, in a two-tiered state like North Carolina, the judge noted, the second-level SRO must give due weight to the first-level ALJ's ruling. In this case, the SRO had rejected most of the ALJ's findings. The district court judge asserted that, although the ALJ's decision may not have been of a high standard, the SRO wrongly swept aside most of the ALJ's findings, which should have been considered correct.

With respect to the assertion of a denial of a FAPE, the district court judge noted the Woods Charter School's provision of modified general physical education was not comparable to the adapted physical education provided in R.S.'s previous IEP. The district court judge ordered the Wake County Public School System to fund private instruction and/or related services of not less than the hours of adapted physical education R.S. should have received but did not because of the charter school's failure to provide. Moreover, the judge ruled R.S.'s parents could choose the provider as long as the provider was licensed or credentialed and their fees were not more than prevailing community rates. This amounted to approximately fifteen hours per week until the end of the 2019–2020 school year. The parents were also to be reimbursed by Wake County Public Schools for travel fees and they could seek attorney's fees. The ruling of the district court regarding the award of compensatory education was appealed to the US court of appeals for the Fourth Circuit.

Ruling:

The three-court panel of the COURT OF APPEALS reviewed the extensive record in this case and found no reason to overturn the district court's compensatory education award. Thus, the court of appeals affirmed the ruling of the district court. A petition was filed to have the case heard by all the judges on the Fourth Circuit Court (a procedure known as en banc), instead of the three-court panel that heard the original case. The appeal for the en banc hearing was denied, so the ruling stood.

Significance to educators:

When a student with an IEP attends a new school within the same district, including a charter school, the new school must provide comparable services. This is also true when a student transfers from a school outside of the district. In *R.S. v. Woods Charter School* the student's previous IEP included adapted physical education, which his IEP team believed was necessary for R.S. to receive a FAPE. The charter school provided a general physical education class with some modifications, which was not comparable to adapted physical education, and thus denied R.S. a FAPE. Because of this denial, the North Carolina school district had to provide compensatory services, related expenses, and attorney's fees.

6.4 Case Summaries from the US Court of Appeals, Fifth Circuit

6.4.1

A.H. v. Austin Independent School District
US Court of Appeals, Fifth Circuit
June 9, 2020
-Unpublished-

Issue:

- Exhaustion of administrative review procedures under the IDEA.

Facts of the case:

A.H., a student with autism, bipolar disorder, and ADHD, attended school in the Austin Independent School District in Texas. He was served in special education and had an IEP providing, among other things, support staff to accompany him throughout the day. A.H.'s mother repeatedly complained to the school district that the aides were not properly trained to provide services to her son.

During an "emotional breakdown" in class, a paraprofessional working with A.H. threw a trash bin at him, which resulted in physical injury and significant dental damage. A.H.'s parents requested a DPH under the IDEA. The parents later added claims against the district under Section 504 and the ADA. The Austin Independent School District argued the IHO lacked jurisdiction over Section 504 and ADA issues. The IHO agreed and dismissed those claims. During the hearing the school district and A.H.'s parents reached a settlement in which the district would pay $50,000 for A.H. to attend a private school of his parents' choice. The parents agreed to drop all IDEA claims while reserving the right to file additional claims under Section 504, the ADA, and Section 1983. The parents subsequently filed suit in federal court under those laws.

The attorneys for the school district argued that, because the new claims involved special education services, they were barred by the IDEA's failure-to-exhaust requirement. The district court agreed, finding the disputes were related to A.H.'s educational needs and thus subject to the IDEA's exhaustion requirement. The claims were dismissed. The parents appealed to the US Circuit Court of Appeals for the Fifth Circuit.

Ruling:

The US Court of Appeals affirmed the lower court's ruling, noting a party is free to pursue claims apart from the IDEA, but must first exhaust the IDEA's remedial process for any such claims that include relief the IDEA can provide. The appellate court thus affirmed the ruling of the US district court.

The appellate court addressed the US Supreme Court ruling in *Fry v. Napoleon* (2017) in arriving at its decision. According to the ruling in *Fry*, if the gravaman, or essence of a complaint, involves a school's failure to provide a FAPE, then exhaustion is required. Thus the exhaustion requirement could not be avoided by bringing the complaint under a different law. The appellate court found A.H.'s parents' pleadings were clearly derived from the school district's failure to provide a FAPE. The court also noted claims solely concerned with physical injury and abuse are not subject to the exhaustion requirements of the IDEA.

Significance to educators:

Parents who have disagreements with a school district regarding the special education and related services provided to their child must exhaust the IDEA's administrative review process before taking their grievances to federal court. According to this court, these exhaustion requirements are not limited to IDEA claims, but also include claims under Section 504 and the ADA seeking relief that is also available under the IDEA.

6.4.2

A.A. & K.K. v. NORTHSIDE INDEPENDENT SCHOOL DISTRICT
US Court of Appeals, Fifth Circuit
March 6, 2020
-951 F.3d 678-

Issues:

- When a student's special education is reasonably calculated to provide a FAPE.
- Procedural violations as a denial of a FAPE.

Facts of the case:

A student, referred to as K.K. by the court, was eligible for IDEA services in the category of emotional disturbance. He had also been diagnosed with pediatric bipolar disorder with psychotic symptoms, autism spectrum disorders, ADHD, mood disorders, and language disorders. Between the ages of three and seven K.K. had been hospitalized on eight occasions.

In kindergarten K.K. had attended school in the Klein Independent School District, where he received his education in a "therapeutic education program." Halfway through second grade K.K transferred to the Northside Independent School District (NISD). His parents alleged the NISD dropped nearly all of his special education services, including counseling, from his IEP. That semester K.K. spent twenty-three days in a hospital and he finished the school year in the Laurel Ridge Treatment Center. When he returned to NISD in third grade he had been diagnosed with the conditions mentioned earlier. K.K.'s admission, review, and dismissal (ARD) team determined he would receive three hours of specialized support a week in a self-contained setting. His IEP did not include counseling services or extended school year services. Later that year K.K. was hospitalized for another twenty-nine days because he exhibited behaviors that indicated self-harm or harming others. At that time K.K. was diagnosed with schizoaffective disorder-bipolar type in addition to his previous diagnoses. K.K. returned to NISD but spent only forty-six days in school the entire academic year. The rest of the time he was hospitalized for suicidal and homicidal ideation. The NISD assessed K.K. on two more occasions and determined he had pragmatic, social, and expressive language disorders. A BIP was written and implemented.

According to K.K.'s parents, the BIP addressed minor issues like blurting out words rather than his more serious behavior problems. The NISD hired an independent evaluator to assess K.K., but the evaluator had to stop the assessment when K.K. became dangerous. K.K.'s parents requested a DPH in which the IHO found in favor of the NISD on all issues raised. The parents filed a complaint against the NISD with the district court for the Western District of Texas. The parents also filed for summary judgment, which was denied. The parents later appealed to the US Court of Appeals for the Fifth Circuit, asking the appellate court to require the NISD to pay for compensatory education.

Ruling:

First, the parents alleged procedural errors on the part of the school district. Finding procedural violations must affect the substantive outcome of the child's IEP, the appellate court ruled any procedural errors committed by the school district did not deny the child a FAPE. Second, the parents also alleged the NISD committed substantive errors. The district acknowledged the Supreme Court's ruling in *Endrew F. v. Douglas County School District* (2017), but used its own four-factor FAPE standard from *Cypress-Fairbanks Independent School District v. Michael F.* (1997) because, as the court noted, "the two (meaning *Endrew F.* and *Cypress-Fairbanks Independent School District*) fit together."

The four factors were: (1) Was the student's educational program individualized on the basis of the student's assessment and performance? (2) Was a student's program carried out in a coordinated and collaborative manner by key stakeholders? (3) Was the student's program in the least restrictive environment? (4) Did the student receive positive academic and nonacademic benefits? Although the district court addressed all four factors, the appellate court only addressed the first and the fourth. Finding the NISD had conducted thorough assessments and K.K. had benefited from special education, the appellate court found in favor of NISD.

Significance to educators:

This court made a distinction between minor procedural errors and serious procedural errors that result in a substantive denial of a FAPE. Special educators should always adhere to the procedural requirements of the IDEA and their state's laws; however, unless these procedural violations impede a parent's right to be meaningfully involved in the special education process or results in a denial of an educational benefit, procedural errors may not result in a denial of a FAPE. As it must, this appellate court relied on the *Endrew F.* decision to determine if K.K. had made progress. The Fifth Circuit court had a four-factor test to determine if a student had received a FAPE. The court determined its four-factor test from its 1997 decision in *Cypress-Fairbanks Independent School District v. Michael F.* conformed to the *Endrew F.* test. Using the four-factor test, the Fifth Circuit Court ruled the NISD had not violated the substantive FAPE provision of the IDEA. In developing a student's program, special educators in the Fifth Circuit should consider if the student's FAPE meets the four-factor test.

6.4.3

Doe v. Harlandale Independent School District
US Court of Appeals, Fifth Circuit
March 11, 2020
-Unpublished-

Issue:

- Exhaustion of administrative review procedures.

Facts of the case:

A parent of a student from the Harlandale Independent School District in Texas asserted the school district had failed to identify her son as needing special education services and thus failed to provide them as required by the IDEA. The parent alleged that, in addition to violating the child-find and FAPE requirements of the IDEA, the school district had violated Section 504 of the Rehabilitation Act and their rights under Section 1983. The parent brought the case directly to the US District Court of the Western District of Texas. The district court dismissed the lawsuit because the petitioner failed to exhaust administrative remedies and had not attempted to show why going through the administrative review process would be futile. The court noted the petitioner needed to exhaust the IDEA administrative review process even if relief was brought under other federal laws (i.e., Section 504, Section 1983). The petitioner filed an appeal with the US Court of Appeals for the Fifth Circuit.

Ruling:

The US court of appeals affirmed the lower court's ruling.

Significance to educators:

This decision has more significance to parents filing complaints against school districts for violations of the IDEA. The appropriate path in resolving such complaints is to go through the administrative review process and only file complaints to the courts following completion of administrative review. In a state with a one-tier administrative process that means going through the DPH and then going to court. In a two-tier state going through the initial DPH and then the state review is important before going on to court. If parents choose to bypass the administrative review process and go straight to court, they bear the burden of proof, which means they will need to prove that bypassing the administrative process was necessary because going through it would have been futile. In such cases school district attorneys would be well advised to challenge the allegation of futility.

6.4.4

P.P. v. Northwest Independent School District
US Court of Appeals, Fifth Circuit
December 14, 2020
-Unpublished-

Issues:

- The child-find requirement of the IDEA.
- School districts' obligation to provide a FAPE.
- Compensatory education as a remedy for the denial of a FAPE.

Facts of the case:

P.P. was a middle school student who attended and received special education services in the Northwest Independent School District in Texas. She had been diagnosed with dyslexia and learning disabilities in reading, math, and writing. On February 1, 2017, an evaluation of P.P. was completed and her IEP was written. A few days later P.P.'s parents, Jennifer and Ray Pinault, informed the school district they were dissatisfied with the IEP and requested an IEE. School district officials granted the request. The IEE was completed on April 5, 2017. Before the IEE was completed, personnel in the school district requested a meeting in order to review P.P.'s IEP. Although the parents refused to attend the meeting, they did agree to amend the IEP without a formal meeting. In May school district personnel and the Pinaults met to revise P.P.'s IEP for the coming year. The IEP committee proposed to add reading, language, math, and writing goals and to enroll P.P. in the school's dyslexia class. The Pinaults rejected the dyslexia class because they did not agree with the school district's teaching method. They specifically wanted P.P. to be taught using the Lindamood Phoneme Sequencing method an independent evaluator had recommended. The Pinaults did not agree to any portion of the IEP.

In June 2017, the Pinaults filed for a DPH, asserting the school district had failed in its child-find duties and FAPE obligations to P.P. They also asked for compensatory education. Prior to the hearing the school district offer another evaluation and individual tutoring. These offers were not accepted by P.P.'s parents. The IHO ruled the school district had violated the child-find obligation from March to October 2016, but had provided P.P. with a FAPE during the 2016–2017 and 2018–2019 school years. The IHO denied compensatory education. Both the Pinaults and school district officials sought review of the IHO's decision in federal district court. The district court judge ruled: (a) the school district violated the child-find obligation from March to October 2016, (b) the school district violated the FAPE obligation during the 2016–2017 school year, (c) the school district satisfied the FAPE requirement in the 2017–2018 school year, and (d) the Pinaults failed to establish an entitlement to compensatory education for P.P. Both parties appealed and cross-appealed to the U.S. Court of Appeals for the Fifth Circuit.

Ruling:

The appellate court applied the standard it had developed in *Cypress-Fairbanks Independent School District* v. *Michael F* (1997) to determine if the Northwest Independent School District had met its FAPE obligations under the IDEA, which the appellate court found met the US Supreme Court's 2017 FAPE standard set in *Endrew F.* v. *Douglas County School District*. The four parts of the test are as follows: (1) Is a student's IEP individualized based on current assessment information? (2) Is it carried out in a coordinated and collaborative manner by key stakeholders? (3) Is it offered in the least restrictive environment? (4) Does it result in academic and nonacademic benefits?

When applying this test the appellate court found the school district's IEPs provided a FAPE, but the district court erred in determining the February 2017 IEP did not provide a FAPE. In an interesting aspect of this ruling, the court replied to school district personnel's refusal to include the Pinaults' insistence on including the Lindamood system in the dyslexia program, which was a general education classroom. In a per curiam opinion, the appellate court judges noted the court respected the school district's discretion to develop its own educational policy for the dyslexia class.

The appellate court found the only compensable IDEA violation the school district committed was the child-find violation, but the Pinaults did not prove a remedy was required. The parents' failure to take advantage of the remedial services offered by the school district and their actions to stymie school district personnel's efforts to correct problems with P.P.'s IEPs also were considered by the court in making the decision about compensatory services. The appellate court affirmed the IHO and district court decision to deny compensatory education.

Significance to educators:

The child-find duties of the IDEA require that if special education personnel know or should have known a child may have a disability and need special education services, they have an affirmative duty to strongly consider conducting a special education evaluation. Furthermore, in situations in which parents disagree with their child's evaluation and/or IEP, school personnel should continue to make good faith efforts to provide the best program they can for the student. In this case school district attorneys undercut the parents' request for compensatory education when they argued the student's parents had failed to take advantage of the remedial services the school district offered and highlighted that student's progress under her IEPs.

6.4.5

R.S. v. Highland Park Independent School District
US Court of Appeals, Fifth Circuit
February 26, 2020
-951 F.3d 319-

Issues:

- School district's obligation to craft an IEP reasonably calculated to provide a FAPE.
- The standard for determining if a school district's IEP confers a FAPE.

Facts of the case:

R.S. was a student with disabilities who was receiving special education services in the Highland Park Independent School District in the Dallas-Fort Worth area. R.S. was nonverbal, nonambulatory, and visually impaired and required assistance in physical activities. The school district conducted a full and individualized evaluation and developed an IEP for R.S. In his IEP, R.S. received services in the following areas: adaptive physical education, assistive technology, augmented alternative communication, music therapy, occupational therapy, physical therapy, special education, and visual impairment. His IEP also included a variety of specialized equipment.

During his five years of attendance he fell five times. His first fall occurred in October 2012. As a result a second teacher or paraprofessional was to be present when he was working with a specialist. After R.S. transferred to a middle school within the school district he fell a fifth time. The school district began holding staff training sessions with R.S.'s teachers and staff to address safety issues when working with him. Additionally, two teachers or staff members were to be with R.S. whenever he was not in his wheelchair. In October 2013 an IEP meeting was held in which the school district acknowledged R.S. had regressed and school district personnel had failed to properly collect data on his progress. School personnel agreed to a new data collection system and to hold monthly meetings with R.S.'s parents, teachers, and service providers.

When discussing compensatory services to be provided to R.S., his parents requested he be enrolled in the Texas School for the Blind and Visually Impaired (TSBVI). School district officials agreed and referred R.S. to the TSBVI program. However, the TSBVI did not accept R.S. for admission because based on its evaluation the student was already receiving a FAPE. The TSBVI did, however, provide consultation and supplemental services through its outreach program. The parents agreed with the new program. In April 2015 R.S.'s parents requested a DPH and provided notice R.S. would be attending a private school, Chase's Place, for the 2015-2016 school year. A hearing was held and in July 2016 the IHO issued a ruling that the Highland Park school district had not violated the IDEA. The ruling denied R.S.'s parents any relief, including expenses associated with his attendance at the private school.

R.S.'s parents filed a complaint with the US District Court for the Northern District of Texas. Both parties filed for summary judgment. In March 2019 the district court issued an opinion granting the school district's motion and denying R.S.'s. The district court in deciding if the Highland Park school district had provided R.S. with a FAPE cited the US Supreme Court's ruling in *Endrew F. v. Douglas County School District* (2017)—to meet the standard of a FAPE, a student's IEP had to reasonably calculated to enable the student to make appropriate progress in light of his or her circumstances. The district court judge used the four-factor FAPE test developed by the US Court of Appeals for the Fifth Circuit in *Cypress-Fairbanks Independent School District v. Michael F* (1997) to determine if the Highland Park Independent School District met its FAPE obligations under the IDEA, which the appellate court found met the US Supreme Court's 2017 FAPE standards. The four-factor test consisted of the following. (1) Was the student's IEP individualized based on an assessment and performance? (2) Was the program administered in the least restrictive environment? (3) Were the services provided in a coordinated and collaborative manner by the key stakeholders? (4) Were positive academic and nonacademic benefits demonstrated?

After applying the four-factor FAPE test, the district court judge ruled the Highland Park school district had provided R.S. with a FAPE as required by the IDEA. The district court judge also found that Texas law, which has a one-year statute of limitations, barred consideration of R.S.'s claims that had occurred more than a year before the DPH request. Additionally, the district court found R.S.'s parents had failed to establish that their son's IEP did not sufficiently ensure his safety. R.S.'s parents appealed to the US Court of Appeals for the Fifth Circuit.

Ruling:

The appellate court reviewed the district court's determination that the school district had provided a FAPE under the IDEA. The judges for the appellate court held any claim challenging the substantive sufficiency of an IEP had to be linked to a specific act adopting, changing, or declining to change the IEP, and such a claim starts when a student's parents know or should have known (the KOSHK standard) that the school district's action resulted in a deficient IEP. In this case this meant an inquiry into when the alleged deficiency became sufficiently apparent that the parents knew or should have known of the problem.

The appellate court also held the district court had properly applied the four-factor FAPE test in determining the school district had provided a FAPE. Moreover, the appellate court agreed with the district court that R.S.'s parents had failed to prove the IEP did not address the student's safety. Further, the appellate court held the Highland Park school district personnel expended a great amount of time and resources developing and implementing R.S.'s IEP and based the IEP on multiple in-depth evaluations of R.S.'s unique needs and abilities with significant input from his parents and expert consultants. R.S. had achieved at least some academic and nonacademic benefits as a result of his plan. The appellate court thus affirmed the ruling of the district court granting summary judgment to the Highland Park school district and denying R.S.'s further claims.

Significance to educators:

Special education providers should use multiple sources of current assessment and student performance data, including information provided by a student's parents, when developing the student's IEP. Additionally, it is crucial that legitimate data are collected on students' performance and be used to inform instruction and programming, and that the IEP be implemented as written. For special educators throughout the United States, the Supreme Court's ruling in *Endrew F.*—requiring a student's IEP be reasonably calculated to enable a student to make progress in light of his or her circumstances—is the FAPE standard that courts and IHOs will apply in hearings and court cases. The FAPE test developed by the US Court of Appeals for the Fifth Circuit in *Cypress-Fairbanks Independent School District* v. *Michael F* (1997) has been used in Fifth Circuit (i.e., Louisiana, Mississippi, Texas) FAPE cases because the appellate court in the Fifth Circuit has held the *Cypress-Fairbanks Independent School District* four-factor FAPE test meets the *Endrew F.* standard. Special educators in the states of Louisiana, Mississippi, and Texas, therefore, may want to consider these four factors (i.e., individualization, least restrictive environment, coordination/collaboration, and academic and nonacademic benefits) when determining if a student's IEP confers a FAPE.

6.4.6

Spring Branch Independent School District v. O.W.

US Court of Appeals, Fifth Circuit

June 12, 2020

-961 F.3d 781-

Issues:

- Child-find requirement of the IDEA.
- Failure to implement a substantial or material portion of a student's IEP as a denial of a FAPE.

Facts of the case:

The parents of O.W., a gifted student with ADHD, mood disorders, anxiety, and oppositional defiant disorder, enrolled him in the Spring Branch Independent School District (ISD) in Texas. As soon as O.W. was enrolled in the school district he began to exhibit problem behavior. The school district conducted an evaluation in order to determine if O.W. was eligible to receive Section 504 accommodations. Because O.W.'s behavior problems worsened and he was failing his classes, O.W.'s mother made an oral request that an evaluation be conducted for special education eligibility. The school district refused to conduct an evaluation. The student's parents paid for a private evaluation.

During this time the school district agreed O.W. was eligible under Section 504 and would receive accommodations. Despite receiving these accommodations, O.W. continued to exhibit problem behaviors and fail classes. He was suspended from school on a number of occasions. About five months after O.W.'s enrollment personnel at his school agreed to conduct a special education evaluation after he assaulted a teacher. While an evaluation was being conducted, school district officials offered O.W. placement in a special program, to which O.W.'s parents agreed. After the evaluation was completed O.W. was deemed eligible under the category of emotionally disturbed. An IEP was developed that included academic and behavioral accommodations.

Close to a month after finding O.W. eligible for services, the school district offered him special education services in the adaptive behavior program at Ridgecrest Elementary School. Despite guidance in O.W.'s IEP to avoid power struggles and to provide him access to a "cooling off" area, staff members at Ridgecrest used timeouts, physical restraints, isolations, and police interventions. The final police intervention proved to be so traumatic to O.W. he was placed on shortened school days for the final month of school.

O.W.'s parents decided to enroll him at a private school, Fusion Academy, for the upcoming school year (2015–2016). They notified the school district in August 2015 of this decision. O.W.'s parents requested a hearing in which they asserted the school district failed to provide O.W. with a FAPE as required by the IDEA. A hearing was held and the IHO ruled (a) the Spring Branch ISD had failed in its child-find duty under the IDEA, (b) the IEP developed for O.W. was appropriate, and (c) the IEP was not properly implemented because the use of physical restraints, timeouts, and police interventions was not consistent with his IEP. The IHO ordered the school district to reimburse O.W.'s parents for two years of tuition at the Fusion Academy because this private school offered appropriate services to O.W. Attorneys for the Spring Branch ISD sue in the US District Court for the Southern District of Texas, alleging the IHO's ruling was inappropriate.

The federal district court ruled that, because the district took more than four months to begin the special education evaluations, despite evidence that O.W. was eligible for services, the IHO's finding regarding the child-find violation was upheld. When examining the IHO's ruling that the school district had failed to implement the IEP, the judge noted O.W.'s IEP focused on positive behavioral supports and teaching of replacement behaviors and did not include the use of timeout, physical restraint, and police interventions as procedures to address O.W.'s problem behavior. The judge also noted a failure to implement a student's IEP may deny the student a FAPE if the failure amounts to a substantial or material failure and more than a minor discrepancy. The federal district court judge found the school district's failure to implement O.W.'s IEP was substantial and denied a FAPE, thus affirming this aspect of the IHO's ruling. The judge also upheld the IHO's award of two years of tuition reimbursement to O.W.'s parents. The district court decision was appealed to the US Court of Appeals for the Fifth Circuit.

Ruling:

The US Court of Appeals for the Fifth Circuit upheld the ruling that the school district had failed in its child-find duties and had not provided a FAPE because of a failure to implement O.W.'s IEP. The federal appellate court remanded the award of remedies to the circuit court.

Significance to educators:

This is an important decision for special education administrators and teachers of students with significant problem behaviors. The child-find duties of the IDEA require that if special education personnel know or should have known (the KOSHK standard) that a child may have a disability and be in need of special education services, they have an affirmative duty to strongly consider conducting a special education evaluation. This is also true if general education interventions, perhaps in a schoolwide MTSS, are not successfully addressing a student's problem behaviors. Additionally, if a student is determined eligible under the IDEA, his or her IEP must address the behaviors using positive behavioral interventions and supports and teach appropriate replacement behaviors. If a crisis intervention plan is in place to be used in the case of extremely disruptive or dangerous behavior, the plan should be included in the student's IEP and be used only if there is an actual crisis. It is extremely important that involved staff understand and implement the student's IEP. Failing to implement the IEP may be a denial of a FAPE.

6.4.7

T.B. v. Northwest Independent School District
US Court of Appeals, Fifth Circuit
November 23, 2020
980 F.3d 1047

Issues:

- Importance of exhausting administrative remedies.
- US Supreme Court's ruling in *Fry v. Napoleon Community Schools* (2021).

Facts of the case:

T.B. was a special student with autism spectrum disorder and ADHD receiving services in the Northwest Independent School District in North Texas. This case arose out of an incident that occurred on April 10, 2017, when T.B. called his mother and requested she pick him up from school. During the call T.B.'s teacher got on the phone and explained to his mother she was losing patience with T.B. After the call T.B. got on a table to avoid his teacher. His teacher reportedly grabbed him and threw him on the ground. She then reportedly dragged him through two classrooms, got on top of him, and, when he got up to run away, kicked him in the chest.

As a result of this incident T.B.'s mother, Jenny Bell, requested a DPH, which was denied because the one-year statute of limitations in Texas had expired. Jenny Bell then filed a complaint with the US District Court for the Northern District of Texas against the school district for failing to provide a safe and nonhostile educational environment and not providing T.B. with an education commensurate with the education his nondisabled peers received. The suit was filed under Section 504 and the ADA. The school district attorneys moved to dismiss the complaint, arguing the plaintiffs had failed to properly exhaust their administrative remedies under the IDEA. The plaintiffs responded that their complaint made no mention of the IDEA or T.B.'s status as a student with disabilities who was receiving special education services. The district court granted the school district's motion, agreeing the court lacked jurisdiction over T.B.'s claims because of his failure to first exhaust his administrative remedies. Eventually T.B. appealed to the US Court of Appeals for the Fifth Circuit.

Ruling:

The appellate court noted that, under the IDEA, a plaintiff must exhaust the administrative procedures (e.g., DPH) before filing a claim under similar laws when the plaintiff's suit seeks relief that is also available under the IDEA. The court also noted the US Supreme Court had addressed the issue in *Fry v. Napoleon Community Schools*, holding the IDEA's exhaustion rule hinges on whether a lawsuit seeks relief for the denial of a FAPE. According to the Supreme Court, if a lawsuit charges a denial of FAPE, the plaintiff cannot escape the exhaustion requirement merely by bringing his or her suit under a statute other than the

IDEA. Similarly, in a suit brought under a different statute, the exhaustion of the IDEA's procedures is not required if the remedy sought is not for the denial of a FAPE. The Supreme Court required that to make this determination a court must determine the essence or gravamen of the issue in the complaint.

According to the Supreme Court, a lower court could determine the gravamen of a complaint by first asking if the plaintiff could have brought essentially the same claim if the alleged conduct had occurred at a public facility that was not a school (e.g., a public theater or library). The court would then ask if an adult at the school (e.g., an employee or visitor) had made essentially the same grievance. If a lower court answers yes to both questions, the claim is not rooted in the denial of a FAPE, and the exhaustion of the IDEA's administrative remedies is not required. On the other hand, if a court answers no to both questions, then the complaint probably does concern a FAPE, even if it does not explicitly say so. Second, the Supreme Court advised lower courts to look to the history of the proceedings, particularly whether a plaintiff has previously invoked the IDEA's formal procedures to handle the dispute, as another possible indicator that the gravamen of the suit is in the denial of a FAPE.

The appellate court observed that T.B.'s use of the IDEA's administrative procedures before filing suit was a strong indicator that the gravamen of his complaint was in the denial of a FAPE, even though the current complaint made no specific mention of a FAPE or the IDEA. In further answering the two questions posed by the Supreme Court in *Fry*, two of the three judges on the appellate court noted that, in a special education setting, the use of physical force as employed by T.B.'s teacher constitutes restraint under Texas state law. School districts do not restrain adult employees or visitors, nor do school districts restrain students outside of the school setting. Therefore, the district argued, the gravamen of T.B.'s claim was more likely to be the denial of a FAPE and thus subject to exhaustion of the IDEA's administrative remedies. Two judges on the appellate court therefore issued a ruling that because T.B.'s complaint sought redress for denial of a FAPE, under the IDEA he was required to exhaust his administrative remedies before bringing a claim to the district court. In a 2–1 ruling, the appellate court agreed with the district court that T.B. had failed to exhaust his administrative remedies and affirmed the district court's ruling in favor of the school district.

One of the three appellate court judges, Judge Stephen Higginson, dissented in this ruling. Judge Higginson noted the case required the court to determine the limits of the IDEA's administrative exhaustion requirement in the context of an allegation of school-based assault. The majority concluded the plaintiff's previous appeal of the IDEA's grievance process, paired with language in the current complaint that appeared to challenge the adequacy of T.B.'s education, provided sufficient grounds to conclude that T.B. was required to exhaust his administrative remedies before filing suit in federal court. Judge Higginson disagreed, asserting the majority of the appellate court overlooked several important principles the Supreme Court had announced in *Fry*.

One of these principles was that in *Fry* the Supreme Court had cited with approval an example provided by the school district to help identify the types of claims not subject to the exhaustion requirement. The Supreme Court explained that if a teacher, acting out of animus or frustration, strikes a student with a disability, the student's claims arising out of that event are unlikely to involve the adequacy of special education and are unlikely to require exhaustion. Moreover, this holds even though the suit could relate to the child's education. Judge Higginson noted the majority did not address this issue, which was a footnote in the Supreme Court's *Fry* ruling, even though the plaintiffs raised this issue. In fact, T.B. sued to challenge the teacher's actions. Even though T.B. was a student with a disability, he did not argue the teacher's response to his disobedience was a misguided attempt to use inappropriate restraints authorized in his IEP; rather, he alleged his teacher's actions were not connected to a legitimate disciplinary purpose and amounted instead to an unprovoked physical assault resulting from animus or frustration. Judge Higginson further wrote that in other court cases, before and after *Fry*, appellate courts throughout the country had similarly held that claims alleging abuse, assault, and harassment, even when suffered by a student with a disability in the school environment, did not require exhaustion. Additionally, Judge Higginson cited other reasons for his dissent in this case.

Significance to educators:

Although this was a 2–1 ruling with a strong dissent, the major takeaway is that in lawsuits involving special education programming, parents must exhaust their administrative remedies before proceeding to court. The exhaustion rule may hold true even though the words *special education*, *IDEA*, or *FAPE* are in the complaint.

6.5 Case Summaries of the US Court of Appeals, Sixth Circuit

6.5.1

Okwuldi Francis CHUKWUANI, M.D. v.
SOLON CITY SCHOOL DISTRICT

US Court of Appeals, Sixth Circuit

April 21, 2020

-Unpublished-

Issue:

- Legal standing of noncustodial parents under the IDEA.

Facts of the case:

The father of a child with an emotional disturbance attempted to legally challenge an Ohio school district's identification of his son as IDEA eligible. An Ohio state court had previously awarded the father's ex-wife exclusive educational decision-making authority on behalf of their son. The father unsuccessfully challenged the school district's evaluation of his son in a DPH. The district court dismissed his complaint appeal based on a lack of legal standing.

Ruling:

The Sixth Circuit agreed with an Ohio district court that the father lacked legal standing to sue. As a result, the Sixth Circuit affirmed the district court's dismissal of the complaint.

Significance to educators:

When a divorced parent who lacks custody of a minor child sues a school district under the IDEA, the school district needs to determine whether the parent retains legal authority to make educational decisions on behalf of the child. If a parent lacks the legal authority to make educational decisions on behalf of their child, they also lack legal standing to file a suit in court.

6.5.2

Keshia CLEMONS, as mother and next friend of T.W. v. SHELBY COUNTY BOARD OF EDUCATION; Scott RICKE; John LEEPER; James NIEHOF, superintendent

US Court of Appeals, Sixth Circuit

June 22, 2020

-Unpublished-

Issue:

- Discrimination based on disability in athletic/extracurricular activities.

Facts of the case:

A parent brought a legal suit against a local school board and school officials on behalf of her daughter, T.W., alleging she had been discriminated against based on her gender and her diagnosis of Asperger syndrome while she was a student-athlete in high school, in direct violation of Title IX, the Rehabilitation Act, and the US and Kentucky constitutions.

T.W.'s parent alleged T.W. was discriminated against based on her disability when she was excluded from the school's tennis team. T.W. had always experienced anxiety and had struggled socially. Based on a psychiatrist's evaluation, T.W. was diagnosed with Asperger syndrome and anxiety. At the time, the parent did not report the diagnosis to the school or request special education services. The high school tennis coach made a statement that he had decided in advance to cut T.W. from the tennis team based on her difficulties with criticism and her uneasiness around him. T.W.'s parent contended the coach's statement supported a finding that he excluded her based solely on her disability-related behaviors.

Ruling:

The Sixth Circuit reversed a judgment in the school district's favor on the parent's Section 504 claim and remanded the case for further proceedings. To prevail on her claim, the parent needed to show that: (1) the student had a disability, (2) the student was otherwise qualified to participate in the school's tennis program, and (3) the coach had denied the student a spot on the team because of her disability. The Sixth Circuit reasoned an individual is otherwise qualified to participate in an activity if he or she can meet program requirements with or without reasonable accommodations. Because T.W. had played tennis for three years and had won three games the year before, the judges noted, she might be "otherwise qualified" if she had accommodations to address her anxiety and difficulty with feedback.

While T.W.'s parents had shown she was treated differently from her peers when she was excluded from the tennis team before tryouts, under the Equal Protection Clause that disparate treatment is acceptable if it was rationally related to some legitimate governmental purpose. The tennis coach asserted he had decided against having T.W. on the team because he was concerned about disruptions and worried another year on the high school tennis team would threaten her emotional and physical safety.

Significance to educators:

School districts need to ensure their athletic coaches do not come to team try-outs with any predetermined decisions regarding which players are going to be cut from a team. Evidence that a coach predetermined whether a student with a disability would make the team could very likely result in a discrimination lawsuit. In this case the tennis coach's statement could support a legal finding that he had excluded the student based solely on her disability.

6.5.3

GARY B., JESSIE K., CRISTOPHER R., ISAIAS R., ESMERALDA V., PAUL M., and JAIME R., minors, plaintiffs v. Gretchen WHITMER et al.

US Court of Appeals, Sixth Circuit

April 23, 2020

Issue:

- Fundamental legal right to basic literacy.

Facts of the case:

Public school students brought this Section 1983 action against the governor of Michigan and other state officials, alleging they had been denied access to literacy on account of their races in violation of their rights under the Due Process and Equal Protection Clauses of the Fourteenth Amendment. The students were enrolled at several of Detroit's lowest-performing public schools. The students blamed their substandard performance on poor conditions within their classrooms, including missing and unqualified teachers, physically dangerous facilities, and inadequate books and materials. Collectively, the students argued these conditions deprived them of a basic minimum education that provides foundational literacy.

Ruling:

The Sixth Circuit held students have a fundamental right to a basic minimum education. The Sixth Circuit explained a right is "fundamental" or protected by the US Constitution if it is: (1) "deeply rooted in the Nation's history and tradition," and (2) so implicit in the concept of ordered liberty that neither liberty nor justice could exist without it. The majority of judges from the Sixth Circuit held the legal right to a basic minimum education met both requirements.

Significance to educators:

Based on this being a decision by the Sixth Circuit, this ruling applies only to public schools in the states of Kentucky, Michigan, Ohio, and Tennessee, but education officials from every state should be aware of its potential impact. The legal recognition of a fundamental constitutional right to a "basic minimum education" means, at the very least, students should have access to foundational literacy. These students claimed they were unable to learn any state-mandated content due to their ongoing difficulties with reading. Those allegations, if proven, could require Michigan officials to step in and ensure all public school students have qualified teachers, safe facilities, and an adequate supply of appropriate and current textbooks.

6.5.4

Jennifer GARZA, individually and as guardian ad litem for C.G. on behalf of C.G. v. LANSING SCHOOL DISTRICT; Connie NICKSON; Tracey KEATON; Martin ALWARDT; Yvonne CAAMAL CANUL; Sheryl BACON; Edna ROBINSON

US Court of Appeals, Sixth Circuit

August 28, 2020

Issue:

- Abuse and neglect of students with disabilities.

Facts of the case:

A parent brought action on behalf of a child under Section 1983 against a school district and its current and former employees, alleging certain school employees bore supervisory liability for a special education teacher's abuse of a student who had autism spectrum disorder and attention deficit disorder. This case arose out of a former special education teacher's physical abuse of a student, C.G. The parent alleged individual school officials bore supervisory liability for the special education teacher's abuse because they were deliberately indifferent to the possibility that the special education teacher had a long history of abusing students.

Throughout the special education teacher's tenure in the school district, employees and community members had repeatedly reported the special education teacher had physically abused students. Employees were trained to report serious teacher misconduct to the school district's human resources department or to their immediate supervisor, who would in turn report it to the human resources department. When employees suspected child abuse, they were also required to file a report with Child Protective Services and to notify the student's parents. According to the parent, however, the administrators only investigated a few of those incidents and generally did not take any remedial measures to prevent further misconduct.

While in class with the special education teacher, the student had asked to sharpen his pencil. The special education teacher refused, but the student proceeded to sharpen his pencil anyway. The student alleged the teacher then grabbed him and pushed him to the floor. The special education teacher maintained he pushed the student to the floor in order to prevent him from using a pencil in a threatening manner.

Ruling:

The Sixth Circuit reversed the dismissal of the parent's Fourteenth Amendment claims against two school principals, reversed a subsequent ruling granting judgment to another three school administrators, and remanded the case for further proceedings. The Sixth Circuit noted in its decision that supervisors are not automatically responsible for employees' constitutional violations. To hold the school administrators liable for the student's injuries, the parent would have to show they knew the teacher was physically abusing his students and failed to take adequate precautions to prevent it from happening again. The Sixth Circuit ruling made clear the school administrators would not necessarily be liable for the special education teacher's misconduct. However, the Sixth Circuit did rule the parent should have the opportunity to pursue her Fourteenth Amendment claims against the school officials named in the lawsuit.

Significance to educators:

Today's school administrators need to know how to respond to ongoing reports that a teacher or other school employee is mistreating a student with a disability. If a school administrator with supervisory authority fails to investigate allegations of student abuse or to take appropriate disciplinary action, they can be considered responsible for those incidents. In this particular case the parent claimed the school administrators disregarded several years' worth of reports that the special education teacher was grabbing, slapping, choking, and throwing students in his special education class. Those allegations, if proven true, could support a legal finding that the school administrators were deliberately indifferent to the likelihood of physical harm.

6.5.5

Cherryl KIRILENKO-ISON; Susan BAUDER-SMITH v. BOARD OF EDUCATION OF DANVILLE INDEPENDENT SCHOOLS

US Court of Appeals, Sixth Circuit

September 4, 2020

Issue:

- Harassment and/or retaliation against school nurses. Adverse employment actions by schools.

Facts of the case:

Two former school nurses brought legal action against a public school board, alleging retaliation under the ADA, Section 504 of the Rehabilitation Act of 1973, and the Kentucky Civil Rights Act, arising out of their advocacy on behalf of two students with diabetes. Based on alleged noncompliance with the medical plan of two students with diabetes, both school nurses discussed filing a complaint with the Cabinet for Families and Children. Both school nurses said they told the local school board about their concerns regarding the students' care, but they received little or no support. Additionally, the superintendent had instructed them not to file a complaint. One of the school nurse's contract was not renewed.

Ruling:

The US Court of Appeals for the Sixth Circuit reversed a district court ruling and granted judgment for the district on the school nurses' Section 504 and ADA retaliation claims and remanded the case for further proceedings. To establish unlawful retaliation, the school nurses needed to show: (1) they engaged in a protected activity, (2) the district knew about that activity, (3) the district took adverse employment action against them, and (4) the protected activity was the reason for the adverse action. As a result, the two school nurses will have a second opportunity to show a Kentucky school district took adverse employment action against them because they raised concerns about the services and accommodations provided to the two students with diabetes.

Significance to educators:

A school nurse's advocacy for certain services or accommodations can legally qualify as a protected activity even if the parent(s) objects to their inclusion in the student's Section 504 plan. School districts need to be aware that any employee reprimands or suspensions resulting from such advocacy may give rise to a retaliation claim under Section 504 or the ADA. In this case the school district argued the program changes the two nurses proposed would amount to "different treatment" and would jeopardize both students' right to a FAPE. Nonetheless, school officials were still required to defend their decisions to suspend one nurse and decline to rehire the second.

6.6 Case Summaries from the US Court of Appeals, Eighth Circuit

6.6.1

*BENTONVILLE SCHOOL DISTRICT v.
Lisa SMITH, as parent of M.S., a minor*

795 F. App'x 992

US Court of Appeals, Eighth Circuit

March 6, 2020

-Unpublished-

Issue:

- Implementation of an individualized education program.

Facts of the case:

A parent brought suit alleging a school district violated the IDEA when it failed to implement a seventh grader's BIP as written and could not challenge a district court ruling in the school district's favor.

Ruling:

The appellate court dismissed the parent's appeal of the implementation issue as moot and otherwise affirmed the district court's ruling that the school district offered the student a FAPE.

Significance to educators:

Courts generally allow parents of IDEA–eligible students to seek compensatory education or other remedies for an alleged implementation failure after the IEP in question has expired. Nonetheless, a school district should still be prepared to show it provided every service in the student's IEP. In this case the school district's evidence of its good faith efforts to implement the student's BIP would have proven valuable if the parent's appeal had been allowed to proceed.

6.6.2

D.L., by next friend Frances LANDON, by next friend MollyJayne LANDON v. ST. LOUIS CITY SCHOOL DISTRICT

950 F.3d 1057

US Court of Appeals, Eighth Circuit

March 2, 2020

Issue:

- Placement under the IDEA.

Facts of the case:

Parents sued on behalf of their child with a medical diagnosis of autism spectrum disorder (ASD) under the IDEA, challenging the state administrative hearing council's decision, which upheld the school district's IEP and school placement. As a remedy, the parents sought tuition reimbursement for a private placement based on the public school district's alleged IDEA violations.

Ruling:

The appellate court affirmed a previous decision by the district court that a student with ASD was denied a FAPE. The Eighth Circuit also reversed a decision by the district court that limited the parents' reimbursement for the student's unilateral private placement. Specifically, the court held the Missouri school district violated the IDEA by failing to offer the sensory supports an elementary school student with autism needed.

Significance to educators:

An IEP team must consider the full range of a student's needs and discuss whether a particular placement offers the support the student requires. In this case not only did the behavioral school lack a sensory room and other autism-related supports, but the school principal testified the school served students who made "poor choices" and needed discipline.

6.6.3

INDEPENDENT SCHOOL DISTRICT NO. 283 v. E.M.D.H., a minor, by and through her parents and next friends, L.H. and S.D.

960 F.3d 1073

US Court of Appeals, Eighth Circuit

June 3, 2020

Issue:

- Eligibility under the IDEA.

Facts of the case:

A school district filed suit, seeking review of an ALJ decision determining a school district denied a student with mental health issues, including depression and anxiety, a FAPE under the IDEA by its failure to identify the student as eligible for special education and related services. The school district argued the high school student with depression, anxiety, and other disabilities was too intelligent to qualify as a student with a disability under the IDEA.

Ruling:

The US Court of Appeals for the Eighth Circuit affirmed a prior decision that the school district denied the student a FAPE under the IDEA. The court also reinstated an administrative order requiring the school district to pay for private tutoring for the student. According to the Eighth Circuit, the Minnesota school district erred in finding the student ineligible for IDEA services based on her above-average academic performance.

Significance to educators:

Whereas an IDEA eligibility team may (and should) consider a student's academic ability when determining the student's need for specialized instruction, it cannot rely solely on academic ability. Instead, the team also needs to consider factors, such as frequent absences and the student's ability to access the general education curriculum.

6.6.4

OSSEO AREA SCHOOLS, INDEPENDENT SCHOOL DISTRICT NO. 279 v. M.N.B., *by and through her parent, J.B.*

970 F.3d 917

US Court of Appeals, Eighth Circuit

July 29, 2020

Issue:

- Entitlement to transportation under the IDEA.

Facts of the case:

A Minnesota school district brought legal action against an open-enrolled student, appealing an ALJ's ruling that the school district was legally required under the IDEA to provide individualized transportation services to the student between the student's home and the school in which the school district had placed the student, as well as reimburse mileage costs.

Ruling:

The US Court of Appeals for the Eighth Circuit held a school district's acceptance of a fifth grade student's open enrollment application did not legally require it to provide home-to-school transportation in the student's IEP. The appellate court thus reversed an earlier district court's ruling requiring the school district to reimburse the parents for all mileage-related costs.

Significance to educators:

No specific IDEA requirement requires a school district to provide transportation services to a nonresident student with a disability who attends a school under an open enrollment program. A school district's obligation to provide transportation to a student with disabilities as a related service will depend on state law.

6.6.5

Chad RICHARDSON, individually, and as parents and next friends of L; Tonya RICHARDSON, individually, and as parents and next friends of L v. OMAHA SCHOOL DISTRICT; Jacob SHERWOOD, superintendent; Amanda GREEN, principal; Dawn DILLON, teacher

957 F.3d 869

US Court of Appeals, Eighth Circuit

April 27, 2020

Issue:

- Procedures for recovering attorney's fees under the IDEA.

Facts of the case:

After an IHO found a school district had failed to conduct necessary evaluations of a student diagnosed with autism spectrum disorder, the parents brought legal action against the school district, seeking an award of attorney fees as the prevailing party of the administrative-level hearing under the IDEA.

Ruling:

The US Court of Appeals for the Eighth Circuit affirmed a prior district court ruling that dismissed the parents' attorney's fee claim as untimely. It also upheld a judgment for the school district concerning the parents' Section 504 and ADA discrimination claims. According to the appellate court, the limitation period for IDEA appeals also applies to attorney's fee claims brought under the federal statute. The Eighth Circuit noted that, while the IDEA gives an aggrieved party ninety days to appeal an unfavorable due process decision, it does not include a specific limitations period for fee claims. This omission has resulted in a current split among the thirteen federal circuit courts of appeal.

Significance to educators:

The US Circuit Court of Appeals for the Eighth Circuit has joined the US Circuit Courts of Appeals for the Sixth and Seventh Circuits in ruling that the limitations period for IDEA appeals applies to attorney's fee claims. School districts located within the Sixth, Seventh, and Eighth Circuits need to keep this rule in mind when evaluating the timeliness of parents' attorney's fee claims. In this case the parents' failure to file within 180 days, or 90 days after the school district's 90-day appeal window had expired, made their attorney's fee claim untimely.

6.7 Case Summaries from the US Court of Appeals, Ninth Circuit

6.7.1

A.L., by and through her guardian, I. LEE v.
CLOVIS UNIFIED SCHOOL DISTRICT et al.

798 F. App'x 163

US Court of Appeals, Ninth Circuit

March 18, 2020

-Unpublished-

Issue:

- Necessary steps involved in the exhaustion of administrative remedies.

Facts of the case:

A guardian appealed a district court's dismissal of claims brought under the ADA and Section 504 of the Rehabilitation Act for failure to exhaust administrative remedies as required by the IDEA. The guardian requested injunctive relief requiring the district to limit the student's segregation from the school's general population and to change its policy of prohibiting aides from communicating with parents. The district court noted integration into general population classes and communication between a school and parents were topics typically discussed when crafting a FAPE.

Ruling:

The appellants did not exhaust IDEA remedies because they settled their IDEA claims without receiving an administrative decision on the merits. Because the appellants' decision to settle in lieu of pursuing IDEA administrative remedies was "clear from the face of the complaint," dismissal was proper.

Significance to educators:

This case involved how much time a student spent in the general education classroom. Although the guardian did not exhaust administrative remedies in this case, districts need to be prepared to defend their actions when the time comes.

6.7.2

BELLFLOWER UNIFIED SCHOOL DISTRICT v. Fernando LUA, individually and on behalf of minor K.L., Sandra LUA, individually and on behalf of minor K.L.

US Court of Appeals, Ninth Circuit

October 26, 2020

-Unpublished-

Issues:

- A school district's obligation to provide a FAPE.
- Whether a private school placement is appropriate.

Facts of the case:

A middle school student with a disability attended a private school outside of the district. Three times the parents requested an IEP meeting. The district stated the parents would have to enroll the student in the district in order for them to develop an IEP. The parents filed a DPH, and an ALJ affirmed the parents had a right to an IEP and were also entitled to tuition reimbursement at the private school despite not providing ten-day notice to the district. The district appealed and the district court affirmed the ALJ decision.

Ruling:

Districts have an obligation to provide a FAPE to eligible students even if a student is attending a private school. The ruling that the district reimburse the parents for the student's private placement was affirmed. The district violated the IDEA by refusing to convene an IEP meeting despite multiple requests from the parents. The regulations specifically state upon a parent's request a district must evaluate a child residing in it for purposes of making a FAPE available, even if the student is enrolled in a private school in another district. Therefore, as the student's district of residence, the district was the LEA responsible for conducting assessments and providing special education services for the student. Additionally, parents may receive reimbursement for the unilateral placement of a child in a private school if the district did not make a FAPE available to the child in a timely manner prior to that enrollment and the private placement is appropriate.

Significance to educators:

An LEA must ensure a child's IEP is reviewed annually and revised as appropriate. This must happen even if the student is attending a private placement. Districts should regularly request of the private placement (with parents' permission) testing and evaluation material in order to keep the present levels of the IEP current.

6.7.3

BUTTE SCHOOL DISTRICT NO. 1 v. C.S.; Stuart MCCARVEL, in his capacity as originator of the C.S. due process complaint

817 F. App'x 321

US Court of Appeals, Ninth Circuit

May 27, 2020

-Unpublished-

Issues:

- A school district's obligation related to procedural violations.
- A school district's obligation related to evaluation of a student for eligibility.

Facts of the case:

During this appeal the caregiver for a former student alleged multiple problems by a school district. First, the caregiver contended the district failed to follow IDEA procedures by not evaluating the student for specific learning disabilities (SLDs), despite staff suspecting he had SLDs in certain academic areas. The caregiver next argued the district did not provide a FAPE because it failed to adequately assess the student's behaviors and develop an appropriate individualized BIP. He further argued the district procedurally erred in its provision of transition services. Finally, he argued the district erred in appointing a guardian for the student when the age of majority was reached.

The district argued it did not evaluate the student for SLDs because the caregiver did not give permission, but it provided accommodations for SLDs. The district stated it had no obligation to conduct an FBA unless it removed the student from his current placement due to behavioral problems. "The record is replete with evidence showing that [district] staff and [the student's] IEP team considered [the student's] problem behaviors and took steps to correct them, including adopting behavioral-intervention plans." Even though the district did not provide transition assessments, it did provide transition services for the student. Finally, the district argued since the student was unable to provide informed consent about his educational program, the district was right to seek appointment of an educational representative. Because the state of Montana had no established procedures in place at the time, the Office of Public Instruction directed the district to seek the appointment of a decision maker using the state's surrogate parent procedure.

Ruling:

The student was not denied a FAPE. The district's obligation to evaluate the student was terminated when the parent did not provide consent. The district also did not have an obligation to develop an FBA on the student. The district, however, erred by not conducting transition assessments and did not appoint the parent as the guardian for the student.

Significance to educators:

Educators must clearly document when parents deny consent for an evaluation. They should also ensure the district closely monitors the behavioral needs of a student and strongly consider an FBA even if the student is not being removed to an alternative placement. Educators should complete a transition assessment as a part of any transition plan. Finally, educators should follow state procedures for the appointment of a guardian but always consider the parent first.

6.7.4

D.D., a minor, by and through his guardian ad litem, Michaela INGRAM v. LOS ANGELES UNIFIED SCHOOL DISTRICT

US Court of Appeals, Ninth Circuit

December 31, 2020

Issue:

- What is necessary to exhaust administrative remedies.

Facts of the case:

The student involved in this case was an elementary school student whose "disability-related behaviors ranged from being off-task and impulsive to being physically aggressive toward peers and adults." During the student's kindergarten year his mother was regularly called to take him home early "because his 'behaviors interfered [with] the other students.'" His mother requested a one-to-one aide in order "to accommodate his needs and enable him to participate with his peers," but the request was denied.

He transferred to a different school for first grade, but his behavior worsened. He struck himself, his classmates, and school staff members. Early in the first grade year his mother was given "an ultimatum": she could either retrieve him from school because of his "disruptive, disability-related behaviors" or have a family member serve as his one-to-one aide in the classroom. Both the mother and her partner worked full-time jobs, but they decided her partner would leave his job so he could serve as the aide. However, late in the school year, on a day her partner was unavailable, the student had a "severe behavioral incident" that prompted the district to summon a psychiatric emergency team (PET). That evening the PET came to the family's home and informed the mother the student needed to be placed on a twenty-four-hour psychiatric hold at a hospital. The student ultimately spent seven days at the facility. After this incident his mother again unsuccessfully requested a one-to-one aide for him. The district continued to say no, stating he could not come to school without a parent (or partner) as an aide. The parent sued, alleging her son was denied access because of his disability.

Ruling:

The more specific factual allegations further indicate the thrust of the student's complaint is his loss of educational opportunity because he was banished from his classrooms, rather than deficiencies in his IEP. Rather than offering meaningful and appropriate behavior accommodations and allowing him to attend school for the same amount of time as his typical peers, the district discriminated against him based on his disability by excluding him from school, refusing to offer an aide, only allowing him to stay in school if his parent served as an aide, and enabling him to be subjected to an unsafe school environment. His disability-caused behavioral issues repeatedly resulted in his removal from school or his classroom, and his mother identified a personal aide as one accommodation she believed reasonable and necessary for her son to obtain the same access to an education as his peers. In other words, she claimed a one-to-one aide would have assisted her son in managing his disruptive behaviors, enabling him to remain in school and in his classroom so he had the opportunity to learn—akin to the access provided by the ramp and the service dog in the *Fry* scenarios. The mother did not have to exhaust her administrative remedies because he was denied access.

Significance to educators:

Districts need to provide a FAPE, but they also need to ensure they are not discriminating against a student. Districts need to be aware of the difference between denial of access and denial of a FAPE. Denial of access can be litigated under Section 504 and the ADA, not just the IDEA.

6.7.5

Esther DE LA FUENTE, on her own behalf and on behalf of A.D. v.
ROOSEVELT ELEMENTARY SCHOOL DISTRICT NO. 66, a political subdivision of the State of Arizona; Jeanne N. KOBA, an individual; Jonathan MOORE, an individual; Freddy MONTOYA, an individual; Cynthia BERNACKI, an individual, and Brent RUSSELL, an individual; KELLY SERVICES, INC., a foreign corporation

US Court of Appeals, Ninth Circuit

July 14, 2020

-Unpublished-

Issue:

- Statute of limitations for Section 504 plan implementation.

Facts of the case:

A parent filed this action for damages on behalf of her son under Section 504 and the ADA. She alleged the school district failed to implement the Section 504 plan from March 2013 to May 2015. The district court granted summary judgment for the district based on the applicable two-year statute of limitations and the parent appealed. The cause of action accrued no later than June 16, 2015, the day she filed the complaint with the OCR. Although the parent could have then filed a parallel civil action for damages in federal court, she filed her complaint two and a half years later, on December 21, 2017.

Ruling:

The claims had become stale. The parent could no longer file since more than two years had passed.

Significance to educators:

Districts should keep track of the specific dates of services and notices to families regarding those services, and they should ensure parents know the dates of those services.

6.7.6

EVERETT H. et al. v. DRY CREEK JOINT ELEMENTARY SCHOOL DISTRICT et al.

799 F. App'x 469

US Court of Appeals, Ninth Circuit

January 9, 2020

-Unpublished-

Issue:

- Whether a case is moot.

Facts of the case:

The student involved in this case was a child with learning disabilities who attended an elementary school in the district. His parents sued the district, its administrators, and the California Department of Education (CDE), asserting violations of the IDEA and related statutes. His parents also brought claims under Section 1983 against California's superintendent of public instruction.

The district court dismissed the Section 1983 claims against the California superintendent. The district court later denied the remaining parties' cross-motions for summary judgment. A trial was then held on the plaintiffs-appellants' claims against the CDE. After the jury found in the CDE's favor on all claims, the parents moved for judgment as a matter of law under Federal Rule of Civil Procedure 50(b) and for a new trial under Federal Rule of Civil Procedure 59(a). The district court denied both motions. The parents then appealed the district court's dismissal of their claims against the California superintendent, from the denial of their motion for summary judgment and from the denial of their posttrial motions.

Ruling:

The US Court of Appeals for the Ninth Circuit dismissed the appeal of the district court's denial of the parents' motion for a new trial. Without a trial transcript, the court could not review the merits of the district court's finding of no prejudicial error. As to the district court's dismissal of the parents' Section 1983 claims against the California superintendent, the court concluded there was no error. Because the student no longer attended school in the district, the claims against the California superintendent in his official capacity were moot. Finally, because the parents did not plead facts establishing the California superintendent had actual or constructive notice of their complaints, they failed to state a claim against him in his individual capacity.

Significance to educators:

Parents may want to retry a case, so make sure everything from previous hearings is covered and the order(s) of the IHO or ALJ are fully implemented.

6.7.8

J.F., a minor, by and through guardians ad litem Aron FEILES and Alexandra FEILES, individually on and on behalf of the proposed class* v. SAN DIEGO UNIFIED SCHOOL DISTRICT, *a government entity

US Court of Appeals, Ninth Circuit

December 15, 2020

-Unpublished-

Issue:

- Exhaustion of administrative remedies.

Facts of the case:

The parents involved in this case were told by the district something to the effect of "please stop filing; we know we don't have aides, and we can't do anything about it." The question was then whether the use of administrative procedures would delay resolution or be futile, and the incident hinted at the inadequacy of the IDEA's dispute resolution procedure. The parents sought the provision of one-to-one aides for only some periods of time. The district had persistent problems with providing aides, and the district court denied the parents' motion, stating they would have to exhaust administrative remedies.

Ruling:

The IDEA's exhaustion requirement did not apply to the student's failure to exhaust administrative remedies. Specifically, exhaustion was not inadequate because the student's claims were not systemic.

Significance to educators:

If parents can demonstrate that exhaustion of administrative remedies would be futile, they may pursue action in other courts.

6.7.9

J.M.; Marla McDONALD v. OAKLAND UNIFIED SCHOOL DISTRICT
804 F. App'x 501
US Court of Appeals, Ninth Circuit
February 21, 2020
-Unpublished-

Issue:

- Attorney's fees.

Facts of the case:

The parent appealed the district court's decision in favor of the district on the question of whether her son was a prevailing party entitled to attorney's fees under the IDEA. The parent argued she had prevailing at an administrative hearing and was therefore entitled to reasonable attorney's fees because the ALJ had ordered the district to (1) provide her son with certain educational records it had previously refused to provide, and (2) locate an interim alternative educational setting for him meeting the criteria developed by their expert witness and witnesses for the district. The district court held these two victories were "technical, de minimis, or ephemeral," and she was therefore not entitled to attorney's fees as a prevailing party.

The IDEA provides that a court, "in its discretion, may award reasonable attorney's fees as part of the costs . . . to a prevailing party who is the parent of a child with a disability" (20 U.S.C. § 1415(i)(3)(B)(i)(I)). A prevailing party is the party who succeeds on any significant issue in litigation that achieves some of the benefit the parties sought in bringing the suit.

To establish prevailing party status under the IDEA, a plaintiff must demonstrate the IHO's order created "a material alteration of the legal relationship of the parties. This means the order must give [the plaintiff] the ability to 'require the district to do something it otherwise would not have to do.'" A plaintiff who obtains relief that is purely technical or de minimis is not a prevailing party. Similarly, a plaintiff who earns only an ephemeral early victory, but who "loses on the merits as the case plays out and judgment is entered against her," is not a prevailing party entitled to attorney's fees.

Ruling:

The US Court of Appeals for the Ninth Circuit affirmed the district court ruling denying the parent's request for attorney's fees.

Significance to educators:

Educators should pay close attention to relief awarded. If the relief is minimal or temporary, then attorney's fees for the parent may either be reduced or not awarded.

6.7.10

K.D., a minor, by and through her guardian ad litem, Leila CARERRA v. LOS ANGELES UNIFIED SCHOOL DISTRICT

816 F. App'x 222

US Court of Appeals, Ninth Circuit

August 12, 2020

-Unpublished-

Issue:

- Whether there is a need to exhaust administrative remedies.

Facts of the case:

In this case the guardian ad litem appealed the district court's dismissal of her action against the district under the IDEA. The district court concluded the student had failed to exhaust the administrative process required by the IDEA because her claim effectively alleged denial of a FAPE. The student was a minor with Prader-Willi syndrome, which produces, among other disabilities, intellectual and speech delays and a sense of hunger that cannot be sated. The student alleged the district never provided teachers and staff with training related to Prader-Willi syndrome, did not conduct an assistive technology/augmentative and alternative communication assessment, did not include important specialists in IEP meetings, and denied her mother's request for a one-on-one aide or the assistance of a behavioral therapist. As a result of the district's alleged failures the student claimed to have suffered a denial of meaningful access to the benefits of a public education, loss of equal educational opportunity, humiliation, hardship, anxiety, depression, and a physical injury. The student requested a DPH under the IDEA to raise her claims, but before the hearing was held, they entered into a settlement agreement. Later the present suit was filed.

Under *Fry v. Napoleon Community Schools* (2017), to determine when claims fall under the exhaustion requirement of the IDEA the Supreme Court explained that the IDEA's exhaustion rule hinges on whether a lawsuit seeks relief for the denial of a FAPE. Two pertinent questions were as follows: (1) Could the plaintiff have brought essentially the same claim if the alleged conduct had occurred at a public facility that was not a school? (2) Could an adult at the school (e.g., an employee or visitor) have pressed essentially the same grievance? The Supreme Court concluded, "when the answer [to those questions] is no, then the complaint probably does concern a FAPE, even if it does not explicitly say so."

Ruling:

The student's claims could only be brought by a student, and only against a school, because they were based on an alleged failure to assess her needs and provide appropriate education to meet those needs. Accordingly, the district court properly held the student had to exhaust her IDEA remedies before seeking judicial relief. The student also argued exhaustion would be futile because she sought monetary damages—which are not available under the IDEA administrative process. The court rejected this argument in *Paul G. v. Monterey Peninsula Unified School District* (2019), where, as here, the damages sought were based on an alleged failure to provide a FAPE.

Significance to educators:

Educators need to ensure parents exhaust their administrative remedies when they have appealed, especially as the case relates to FAPE.

6.7.11

L.F., in his individual capacity and as parent of K.S.F (Student 1) and K.S.F. (Student 2); K.S.F., Student 1; K.S.F., Student 2 v. *LAKE WASHINGTON SCHOOL DISTRICT #414*

US Court of Appeals, Ninth Circuit

January 17, 2020

947 F.3d 621

Issue:

- Parents' First Amendment rights relating to complaints.

Facts of the case:

The parent involved in this case contended his daughters suffered from anxiety and behavioral disorders that adversely affected their educational performance. He had several disagreements with district personnel regarding (1) the best ways to address these issues and (2) what he saw as discrimination against him as a divorced father. For its part, the district contended that, beginning in March 2015, the parent engaged in a pattern of sending incessant emails to staff accusing them of wrongdoing, making presumptuous demands, leveling demeaning insults, and acting in an aggressive, hostile, and intimidating manner during face-to-face interactions. District employees complained the parent's extraordinarily time-consuming communications made district staff feel threatened and intimidated.

The district imposed a communication plan. The terms of the plan were spelled out in an email to the parent. Under the plan the parent's substantive communications with the district about his daughters' education would be limited to biweekly, in-person meetings with an administrator. The parent was advised not to email or attempt to communicate in any form with any district employees aside from the biweekly meetings, "as they will not respond to [his] emails or attempts to communicate."

The communication plan's restrictions did not apply in the event of an emergency, did not affect the parent's right to appeal the decision regarding the Section 504 plan, and did not bar him from attending school activities or accessing school records. The parent was told he had a right to challenge the communication plan by filing an appeal in state court. The parent claimed the communication plan violated his First Amendment rights.

Ruling:

The communication plan did not restrict the parent's right to advocate on the students' behalf, just the frequency of the communication.

Significance to educators:

Educators should make sure parents have an opportunity to participate, to be heard, and to voice concerns about a program.

6.7.12

Lexyington McINTYRE v. EUGENE SCHOOL DISTRICT 4J, and Cheryl LINDER; Andy DEY; Michael STASACK; Susie NICHOLSON; Suzie McLAUCHLIN

US Court of Appeals, Ninth Circuit

September 23, 2020

796 F.3d 902

Issues:

- Necessary steps to exhaust administrative remedies.
- When a Section 504 plan is appropriate.

Facts of the case:

In early 2012, during the seventh grade, the student was diagnosed with attention deficit disorder (ADD). The district accordingly developed a Section 504 plan for the student that had limited accommodations, including extra time on tests and assignments, reduced assignments and projects, preferred seating, and a quiet and separate testing environment.

In fall 2013 the student started as a high school freshman in a French immersion program and enrolled in a French-language program with teacher Michael Stasack. But Stasack declined to implement the student's Section 504 plan accommodations and repeatedly suggested she did not belong in the program due to her ADD. At the end of the school year in May 2014, the parents filed a formal "Bullying/Harassment" complaint against Stasack with the district. The district investigated and found two violations of its discrimination and harassment policies. The student suffered from post-traumatic stress disorder because of the discrimination and harassment she faced that year. As a remedy for the violations, the district offered options for addressing the language class.

The student's junior year was especially challenging. At the beginning of the eleventh grade in fall 2015, she was diagnosed with Addison's disease, a rare hormone condition. The district accordingly amended the Section 504 plan to include an emergency protocol that required the district to call 911 if she were seriously injured. In addition, because of the disease, the student could no longer take her ADD medication.

As to the student's language study, after the district discouraged her from taking college courses, the student began a district independent study program for the 2015–2016 school year. The instructor was Suzie McLauchlin, a non-language teacher who was not certified to administer International Baccalaureate exams and was not accredited to teach Advanced Placement (AP) courses. McLauchlin rarely met with the student. As the school year progressed the student lacked sufficient opportunity to practice French and she was unprepared for the AP exam in spring 2016.

Among her other teachers, the student's math teacher, Susie Nicholson, also repeatedly declined to implement the Section 504 plan accommodations.

Nicholson declined to provide the student with testing accommodations, forcing her to take exams in a way that was embarrassing to her or left her with less time on the exams than her peers. Nicholson's actions further contributed to the student's stress and anxiety and exacerbated her Addison's disease.

Toward the end of the student's junior year in spring 2016, the district reassigned Stasack to a different school after it investigated another student's complaint against him. The student's peers in the French immersion program organized a walkout to protest Stasack's reassignment. They also protested the accommodations students with disabilities sought, believing Stasack was "fired because of the 504 kids." With McLauchlin's permission, students walked out of McLauchlin's social studies class on May 26, 2016. The student felt isolated from her peers and betrayed by McLauchlin and the district administrators who failed to intervene. Throughout the following year, the student's classmates maintained their resentment, harassing and bullying her for her perceived role in Stasack's transfer. They ultimately designed a sweatshirt celebrating him, which students wore at their graduation ceremony in 2017. District officials never addressed the hostile learning environment the student experienced.

In June 2016 the student fractured her ankle during a physical education class. Despite the Section 504 plan's emergency protocol requiring district officials to call 911, district officials declined to call for an ambulance. Additionally, during her 2016–2017 senior year the district made it difficult for the student to apply for college because of her disability. A case was filed alleging violations of Section 504 and Title II. It was dismissed because she had not exhausted her administrative remedies.

Ruling:

The crux of the student's complaint sought relief for the disability-based discrimination and harassment she faced at school, and not for the denial of a FAPE under the IDEA. As a result the student need not exhaust the administrative remedies under the IDEA. The student first complained the district discriminated against her by failing to provide her with specific accommodations, none of which constituted FAPE as the IDEA defines it. The student's complaint alleged the district failed to (1) provide an alternative, quiet location to take exams, (2) provide extra time to complete exams, and (3) comply with an emergency health protocol. These accommodations cannot be construed as "special education" because they do not provide "specially designed instruction."

Significance to educators:

The *Fry* rule only applies when a student seeks relief for a denial of a FAPE as defined by the IDEA.

6.7.13

Terria McKNIGHT v. LYON COUNTY SCHOOL DISTRICT
US Court of Appeals, Ninth Circuit
July 8, 2020
-Unpublished-

Issues:

- School districts' obligations related to providing FAPE.
- Necessary components of an IEP.
- When a paraprofessional should provide services for a child.

Facts of the case:

In this decision a parent alleged first that a school district had inappropriately allowed an autism specialist to observe her child. Second, the district failed to provide the student a one-on-one aide in general education classes. Third, the district did not provide appropriate progress monitoring details on the student. Fourth, the district violated the student's right to privacy by allowing a newspaper picture of the student while in school.

Ruling:

The US Court of Appeals for the Ninth Circuit affirmed the district did not violate the IDEA when an autism specialist conducted an observation of the student because the observation was a "screening of a student by a teacher or specialist to determine appropriate instructional strategies" and did not require parental consent under the IDEA.

Additionally, it affirmed the determination that the district did not deny the student a FAPE by failing to provide him a one-on-one aide in the general education classroom because the student's IEPs were "reasonably calculated to enable [him] to achieve passing marks and advance from grade to grade." It also affirmed the determination that the district did not deny the student a FAPE by failing to provide the parent sufficient information about the student's progress because the student's IEPs complied with IDEA requirements and the district did as they specified and more. Finally, judgment was appropriate when a newspaper photographer took the student's photograph in the cafeteria because the parent failed to raise a triable dispute as to whether the district deprived the student of any constitutional right.

Significance to educators:

Educators should keep data on students' needs and make sure the data address the specifics of the services they may require in special education as well as in the general education classroom.

6.7.14

N.G., a conserved adult, by and through her conservators, R.G. and G.G. et al. v. PLACENTIA YORBA LINDA UNIFIED SCHOOL DISTRICT

807 F. App'x 648

US Court of Appeals, Ninth Circuit

April 6, 2020

-Unpublished-

Issue:

- When a residential placement is necessary for a student.

Facts of the case:

In this decision the student was a young woman on the autism spectrum who qualified under the IDEA because of her significant intellectual deficits. Until 2016 the district funded her attendance at a certified nonpublic school. In September 2015 the parents asked the district to offer the student a placement in a full-time residential treatment program because the behavioral progress she had made at school was not reflected at home, where her self-injurious and aggressive behavior continued and negatively affected her twin sister, who also had significant disabilities. This request was denied. The parents alleged the failure to offer the student a residential placement denied her a FAPE for the 2014–2015 and 2015–2016 school years. In January 2016 the parties entered into a settlement in which the district agreed to help fund the student's unilateral placement at Heartspring, a private residential treatment center in Kansas, through June 2016. The agreement also provided that the parties would proceed with an annual meeting to develop an IEP for the student for the 2016–2017 school year "to offer [her] an IEP for the period following expiration" of their settlement agreement. During that meeting the district again did not offer the student a residential placement, and shortly thereafter the parents enrolled her at Heartspring. The agreement was ultimately extended to provide a total of $145,000 in funding through December 31, 2016.

In a DPH the ALJ found the student had failed to meet the burden of establishing that, during any time period at issue in this case, she required a residential placement for educational purposes, or that placement at a nonpublic school would not provide her with a FAPE. The ALJ found "the weight of the evidence . . . demonstrated that student had been making significant educational and behavioral progress" prior to her parents' unilateral placement at Heartspring. The parents appealed the denial of residential placement.

Ruling:

The US Court of Appeals for the Ninth Circuit affirmed the factual determination that there was no relevant time when a residential placement of the student was necessary to provide special education and related services.

Significance to educators:

The determination of whether a student requires residential services rests on whether progress is being made in a day program, not on progress in the home. Educators should keep good progress-monitoring measures to assist in this determination.

6.7.15

Regina Marie PANGERL, individually and on behalf of T.P. v. PEORIA UNIFIED SCHOOL DISTRICT

806 F. App'x 553

US Court of Appeals, Ninth Circuit

March 25, 2020

-Unpublished-

Issue:

- Whether a student was enrolled in a program.

Facts of the case:

The student involved in this case had been receiving special education services from the district since preschool. The parent alleged the student was enrolled to attend twelfth grade during the 2013–2014 school year in the district, but that the district unilaterally disenrolled the student from the school due to unexcused absences. At the time the district disenrolled the student, she had an existing IEP and there was a pending due process proceeding related to her IEP. The parent decided to place the student in a private school for the 2013–2014 school year after the district disenrolled the student. Later in the school year, however, the student was hospitalized, and the parent contacted the district, requesting it provide the student homebound services. The district replied it was "not obligated to [provide] FAPE" because the parent had placed the student in a private school.

Based on these allegations the due process complaint asserted, among other things, that the district denied the student a FAPE when it (1) took affirmative, unilateral action disenrolling the student from the school and (2) refused to provide homebound services. During oral argument the district clarified that disenrolling the student meant there was a "change in [her] status at the school" and that the student would be unable to attend the school until her parents came to the school and asked to reenroll the student. The parent's due process complaint thus alleged that, based on the district's disenrollment of the student, she was prevented from attending the school, thereby denying her a FAPE. The due process complaint additionally asserted the district violated the IDEA's stay-put requirement because it disenrolled the student from school while there was a pending due process proceeding relating to her existing IEP. The ALJ and the district court dismissed the parent's DPH complaint and the parent appealed.

Ruling:

The US Court of Appeals for the Ninth Circuit affirmed the right to a DPH on the merits of the case. It remanded the case to be heard and expressed no view as to the actual merits of the parent's claims.

Significance to educators:

Educators must honor stay-put claims. They cannot disenroll students for whom the district should still be providing an education.

6.7.16

SAVE ACCESS ACADEMY, an unincorporated association v. MULTNOMAH COUNTY SCHOOL DISTRICT NO. 1J, an Oregon public corporate entity by and through the Board of Directors of Multnomah County School District No. 1J; Guadalupe GUERRERO, Superintendent, individually and in his official capacity

804 F. App'x 690

US Court of Appeals, Ninth Circuit

May 6, 2020

-Unpublished-

Issues:

- Whether a student was discriminated against because of disability.
- Determining the least restrictive environment for a student.

Facts of the case:

Save Access Academy (SAA) argued a district violated its Fourteenth Amendment right to due process by splitting the academy into two separate school buildings. As the district court cut correctly concluded, SAA lacked a protected property interest in the academy as a single-site program. The district court dismissed its Section 1983 due process claim.

Save Access Academy next contended that dividing ACCESS Academy into two buildings violated the ADA's integration mandate. In its view the division discriminated against students with disabilities by hindering their ability to interact with their nondisabled peers. The district asserted the division of the program was by age with elementary school-aged students going to the elementary school and middle school-aged students going to the middle school.

Ruling:

Because the division separated elementary school students from middle school students, it in no way segregated students with disabilities from their nondisabled peers. As a result, the school district cannot be held liable for discrimination under the ADA.

Significance to educators:

School district personnel should make sure they do not unnecessarily separate students with disabilities from their same-age peers, and they should make every attempt to ensure students with disabilities interact with their nondisabled peers.

6.8 Case Summaries from the US Court of Appeals, Tenth Circuit

6.8.1

Donahue v. *Kansas Board of Education*

US Court of Appeals, Tenth Circuit

September 14, 2020

-Unpublished-

Issues:

- Procedural errors may violate the FAPE provisions of the IDEA.
- When bringing a lawsuit under the IDEA the party bringing the lawsuit must exhaust administrative remedies.

Facts of the case:

The plaintiff in this case, Toni Donahue, filed a *pro se* action against the Olathe School District.[2] The plaintiff did not believe the school had met its obligations to her child under the IDEA and requested a DPH. The attorneys for the school district argued Ms. Donahue's due process complaint omitted required information and should therefore be dismissed. The IHO agreed and dismissed Ms. Donahue's due process complaint as insufficient. Ms. Donahue appealed the dismissal to a SRO who also ruled against her. Ms. Donahue then appealed to the US District Court in Kansas. The district court dismissed Ms. Donahue's claims and she filed an appeal with the US Court of Appeals for the Tenth Circuit.

Ruling:

The circuit court noted multiple procedural errors in Ms. Donahue claim, and she had also failed to properly raise several issues on appeal. The appellate judges explained that as an appellate court, it could only review claims brought up in the plaintiff's brief. If the mother did not raise a claim in her initial appellate brief, it continued, she waived that claim or lost the opportunity to appeal it. Because the mother filed the appeal without a lawyer, the US Court of Appeals for the Tenth Circuit explained, it would overlook certain errors and give the mother the benefit of the doubt in terms of bringing claims on appeal. However, even after giving her brief the benefit of the doubt, the appellate court judges concluded the mother did not actually challenge the district court's dismissal of her complaint for lack of subject matter jurisdiction because she failed to exhaust her administrative remedies under the IDEA. Accordingly, it concluded she had lost her ability to challenge that decision.

---

2. The litigant or parties represent themselves in a DPH or court without the assistance of an attorney.

Significance to educators:

The significance of this case may be that it shows the potential of going to DPH *pro se*. It also shows that a school district's attorneys may succeed in limited appeals by challenging a parent who fails to meet parts of a court's order.

6.8.2

Elizabeth B. v. El Paso County School District 11

US Court of Appeals, Tenth Circuit

December 16, 2020

-Unpublished-

Issues:

- Conducting FBAs and implementing BIPs.
- The importance of addressing concerning student behavior in IEP meetings.
- The Burlington Carter test for tuition reimbursement.

Facts of the case:

The parents of a six-year-old student called Lizzie who had autism and epilepsy enrolled her in Madison Elementary School in El Paso County School District in Colorado Springs, Colorado. During unstructured times during the school day, Lizzie exhibited noncompliant, self-injurious, and self-stimulating behaviors. The school proposed an IEP for Lizzie that included fifteen hours of special education services per week, with additional hours for speech and language services and physical and occupational therapy. Her parents rejected the IEP and asserted because it lacked a BIP, applied behavior analysis (ABA) therapy, and extended school year (ESY) services it did not provide FAPE. The parents enrolled her in a private school and filed a complaint requesting the school district reimburse them for tuition at the private school. A DPH was held, and the ALJ ruled the IEP provided a FAPE and that Lizzie's parents were not entitled to relief. The parents appealed to the US District Court for the District of Colorado, which affirmed the ALJ's ruling. Lizzie's parents then appealed to the US Court of Appeals for the Tenth Circuit.

Ruling:

Lizzie's parents made the following arguments to the circuit court. First, her IEP was fatally flawed because it did not include an FBA and a BIP. The circuit court pointed out the IDEA does not require the team to create a specific intervention plan—rather the law only requires that the IEP team consider positive behavioral interventions and supports when a student's behavior impedes his or her own learning and the learning of others. According to the circuit court, the IEP team did consider the behaviors but found a behavior plan unnecessary. Moreover, the court found Lizzie's parents had failed to prove her behaviors interfered with her learning or the learning of others and noted the problem behaviors only occurred during unstructured times (e.g., recess) and quickly subsided when she was in the classroom. The circuit court further found that, although no formal plan was developed, the IEP team did begin drafting a tip sheet for Lizzie's teachers to help them identify and respond to problem behaviors.

Lizzie's parents also argued the school district had failed to provide a FAPE because it did not include ABA therapy in her IEP. The circuit court rejected the ABA argument because the school district included behavioral strategies that effectively addressed Lizzie's problems and was not required to use the parents' preferred label. The parents also asserted there was abundant evidence that Lizzie needed ESY services. However, the circuit noted the IEP team decided ESY services were not needed and Lizzie's parents did not provide evidence of her need for ESY services. Because the IEP did provide a FAPE, the parents were not entitled to reimbursement for placing Lizzie in a private school. The circuit court affirmed the decision of the district court.

Significance for educators:

Elizabeth B. v. El Paso County School District (2020) was a tuition reimbursement case. In such cases, if parents unilaterally remove their IEP–eligible child from the public school and place him or her in a private school, the parents may later seek reimbursement for tuition and related expenses under the US Supreme Court's Burlington/Carter test. In this test the court determines if the public school failed to provide a FAPE, if the private school had provided an education that met a student's needs, and whether equitable considerations warranted reimbursement in full or part. In this case it was determined that the school provided the students with a FAPE, so the court did not need to address the second and third parts of the test.

A significant part of this case involved the student's behavioral problems. The parents asserted Lizzie had not received a FAPE because her IEP did not include a BIP. The circuit court noted the IDEA does not mandate a specific BIP. Rather it requires that the team address behavioral issues and include positive behavior interventions and supports to address the behavior when that behavior interferes with a student's learning or the learning of others. In this situation the team had decided Lizzie's behavior did not interfere with her learning or that of others because problem behaviors occurred during unstructured times and ceased during classroom activities. Additionally, the team was developing a behavior tip sheet for general educators so they could recognize and appropriately respond to problem behavior. We advise that behavior information of this nature be included in a student's IEP as a program modification.

6.8.3

Board of Education of Gallup-McKinley County Schools v. Native American Disability Law Center

US Court of Appeals, Tenth Circuit

May 19, 2020

Issue:

- Time lines for recovering attorneys' fees.

Facts of the case:

The Gallup-McKinley school district in Gallup, New Mexico, filed an IDEA claim in order to recover attorney's fees from a student's parent, Mavis Yazzie, who had filed a suit against the Gallup-McKinley school district and the New Mexico School for the Deaf. The Gallup-McKinley school district convinced the IHO to dismiss the district from the due process complaint. The school district also sued the student's parents in order to recover attorney's fees the district had incurred in defending itself. Because New Mexico has a specific time frame for requesting attorney's fees following an administrative hearing, which the district had apparently exceeded, the US District Court dismissed the district's petition as untimely. The state had a thirty-day statute of limitations on seeking attorney's fees, which began the day the IHO issued his final opinion. The school district attorneys had filed their petition within thirty days of the final decision, but the judge determined meeting the requirements of the law meant the school district should have filed the petition when it was removed from the case. The school district appealed to the US Court of Appeals for the Tenth Circuit.

Ruling:

The circuit court recognized the school district hadn't filed its petition until twelve weeks after the district was removed from the case; nonetheless, the court ruled the school district's claim was timely because the thirty-day limitation did not begin until the parties received the IHO's final decision. The circuit court reversed the district court's decision and remanded the case for further procedures.

Significance to educators:

The case has direct significance to educators in New Mexico. The case should also serve as an alert to prevailing parties in DPHs under the IDEA to know their state's time lines for filing for attorney's fees.

6.9 Case Summaries from the US Court of Appeals, Eleventh Circuit

6.9.1

Christopher GLOSTON, by Tamika GLOSTON, his next friend, parent, and natural guardian v. Jack VANCE

789 F. App'x 845

US Court of Appeals, Eleventh Circuit

January 10, 2020

-Unpublished-

Issue:

- Abuse and neglect of students with disabilities.

Facts of the case:

A parent filed a complaint against a teacher, the school board, and the district on behalf of her son who had multiple disabilities, including cerebral palsy, which relegated the student to a wheelchair. The suit alleged a teacher placed a towel over the student's head, put him in a choke hold, and struck him in the face with his hand. The parent claimed the teacher violated the Fourteenth Amendment by engaging in conduct that was shocking to the conscience and also violated the student's due process rights. The teacher claimed he placed a towel over the nonverbal teenager's head during a field trip to stop him from screaming.

Ruling:

The US Court of Appeals for the Tenth Circuit vacated the district court's ruling, denied the teacher's motion for judgment, and remanded the case for further proceedings. According to the appellate court, the district court should have taken the record of facts in the light most favorable to the student. It then should have considered whether the teacher violated the student's constitutional rights and whether those rights were clearly established.

Significance to educators:

Factual disputes over whether a teacher's behavior management techniques qualify as abuse and mistreatment of a student with a disability will not necessarily preclude a judgment in the teacher's favor. Instead, a court must consider (1) whether the teacher's purported misconduct violated the student's constitutional rights and if so (2) whether those rights were clearly established at the time. In this case the district court's failure to address these two questions required it to reconsider whether the teacher was immune from suit.

6.10 Case Summaries from the US Court of Appeals, DC Circuit

6.10.1

Sanchez & Z.B. v. DISTRICT OF COLUMBIA PUBLIC SCHOOLS

US Court of Appeals, DC Circuit

May 15, 2020

-Unpublished-

Issues:

- Procedural errors may violate the FAPE provision of the IDEA.
- The importance of involving parents in all special education decisions.

Facts of the case:

A student in special education, Z.B., attended a private school in Washington, DC, the Kingsbury Day School. The DC public school district sought to transfer Z.B. to another private school, the Kennedy Krieger Institute. K.B.'s mother, Sylvia Sanchez, asserted the transfer to the new school would violate Z.B.'s right to a FAPE under the IDEA. K.B.'s mother blocked the transfer, began paying K.B.'s tuition at the Kingsbury Day School, and sought tuition reimbursement. The mother also contended the transfer to the day school did not involve K.B.'s parents and thus constituted improper predetermination. A DPH was held. The IHO ruled K.B.'s mother was given numerous opportunities to provide input into her son's placement but refused, therefore the school district had not violated her right to be involved in the decision. Because K.B.'s mother had not raised her issues with her son's IEP in the hearing, those issues were not considered. K.B.'s mother filed an appeal with the US District Court in Washington, DC. The district court, in finding for the school district, ruled any procedural violations were harmless. The case was appealed to the US Court of Appeals for the DC Circuit.

Ruling:

The circuit court affirmed the district court ruling that the parent was not entitled to reimbursement for the cost of maintaining the student's initial nonpublic placement. In the ruling the circuit court focused on whether the alleged placement change violated the parent's right to participate in the placement process. Although K.B.'s mother argued she was excluded from placement discussions, which might have entitled her to relief for the alleged procedural violation, the circuit court noted the district encouraged the parent to (a) visit the proposed school, (b) allow the student to visit the school, and (c) provide input on possible schools for the student. Because the DC districts had made good faith efforts to work with the mother, the court found any alleged procedural violation harmless.

Significance to educators:

When school personnel consider a change of placement, it is very important that a student's parents be involved in the decision-making process. In this case the school district had made good faith efforts to include the boy's mother and documented all these efforts. Moreover, the documentation undermined the parent's claim that she was left out of discussions by showing that school district personnel encouraged her to visit the proposed school and repeatedly attempted to meet with her. The lesson to educators is to document, document, document!

6.10.2

Keith Allen, et al. v. DISTRICT OF COLUMBIA
US Court of Appeals, DC Circuit
August 11, 2020

Issues:

- The IDEA allows the prevailing parties in a special education lawsuit to collect attorney's fees.
- The calculation of the amount of attorney's fees in Washington, DC.

Facts of the case:

Washington, DC, passed the DC Appropriations Act in 2009. The law prohibited the District of Columbia from paying more than $4,000 in a single IDEA–related action. The Washington, DC, school district had long struggled to comply with IDEA requirements. These struggles led to a flurry of IDEA lawsuits. For example, in 1998 the school district was paying more than $10 million per year in attorney's fees for special education lawsuits. Congress responded to this problem by passing a series of appropriations riders that limited the amount the district could pay out of current appropriations. One of these riders prohibited the DC district from paying more than $4,000 per proceeding out of current appropriations for IDEA attorney's fees. Parents who prevailed against the DC district in IDEA proceedings initiated before the 2009 act was enacted were awarded attorney's fees. The DC district, however, refused to pay fees that exceeded the cap of $4,000 per proceeding. In 2015 the plaintiffs moved to compel the DC district to pay the balance of their attorney's fees with interest. The district court held the 2009 act applied to all the plaintiffs' IDEA proceedings. A magistrate judge then determined the DC district owed a total of about $3.7 million in fee awards and more than $1.3 million in interest. He did not recommend the DC district be required to pay any interest.

Both sides filed objections to the magistrate judge's report and recommendation. The plaintiffs asserted the DC district should be required to pay interest on the full amount of fee awards, not just on amounts up to the payment cap. The DC district responded it could not be compelled to pay interest on debts it was legally forbidden to pay off. The district court agreed with the plaintiffs. It held the DC district's position was meritless and required it to pay about $220,000 in further outstanding fee awards, which were limited by the payment cap, and about $1.4 million in interest accumulated on the entire amount of all unpaid awards.

Ruling:

The DC Circuit Court reversed the decision that required the district to pay parents a combined $1.4 million in interest and remanded the case for further proceedings. It also affirmed the district court's decision that the appropriations act was constitutional and applied retroactively. This ruling did not relieve the DC school district of its obligation to pay post-judgment interest on legal fees owed to parents who had prevailed in IDEA actions. The district only had to pay post-judgments interest on fee awards up to $4,000—the maximum amount it could pay to any prevailing parent under the 2009 act.

Significance to educators:

This ruling only applies in Washington, DC. Administrators and educators nonetheless need to be aware that funds that could otherwise be spent on the education of students with disabilities may be expended on attorney's fees and related expenses when they violate the requirements of the IDEA.

6.10.3

J.T. v. DISTRICT OF COLUMBIA
US Court of Appeals, DC Circuit
December 29, 2020

Issue:

- A FAPE case was ruled to be moot. Federal courts only have constitutional authority to resolve actual disputes, so legal action cannot be brought in these courts if the situation has been resolved and there is no case left for the court to settle.

Facts of the case:

The plaintiff in the case, J.T., asserted the Washington, DC, school district had failed to offer her son, V.T., a FAPE based on his 2017 IEP. She filed a DPH but before the hearing was held the DC school district agreed to fund V.T.'s attendance at a private school, so J.T. no longer sought retrospective relief. When the hearing took place the IHO ruled the current IEP provided V.T. a FAPE, thus ruling for the school district. J.T.'s parents then filed an appeal with the US District Court, which ruled that because the 2017 no longer controlled V.T.'s education and J.T. had not filed for retrospective relief, the case was moot. The mother appealed to the US Court of Appeals for the DC Circuit.

Ruling:

Rather than seeking relief the parents asked for a declaration that the 2017 IEP was inadequate and to change the 2018 IEP to the requested specifications. In an attempt to avoid dismissal because of mootness, J.T. argued a declaratory judgment would provide relief because the prior IEPs helped establish baselines for future IEPs. The judges asserted the boy's 2017 IEP would not serve as a baseline for future IEPs because the school district and parents had agreed to changes to the 2017 IEP. Since the case presented a fact-specific appeal to an IEP that was no longer operative, the parties had subsequently agreed to a new IEP, and J.T. did not seek retrospective relief, the circuit court affirmed the ruling of the district court that the case was moot.

Significance to educators:

School district personnel may avoid litigation by addressing the evolving needs of students and parental concerns. If a student is not progressing, changes to meet a student's needs must be made. Furthermore, meaningful data should be collected to monitor the student's progress.

Glossary of Legal Terms

Administrative appeal: A quasi-judicial proceeding before an independent hearing officer or administrative law judge.

Administrative law judge (ALJ): Some states use administrative law judges (ALJs) appointed by the state to conduct due process hearings in special education cases. In most states an ALJ may conduct administrative hearings in several areas (e.g., special education, labor relations, housing, insurance). An individual presiding at an administrative due process hearing has the power to administer oaths, hear testimony, rule out questions of evidence, and make determinations of fact. The role of an ALJ in IDEA proceedings is like that of an independent hearing officer, with some small differences among the states.

Adversary process: The methods used in hearings and court cases whereby each side presents its case to the hearing officer or judge. The presentations of both sides are subject to the rules of evidence. The hearing officer or judge is the independent fact finder who determines whose evidence is more persuasive and which party prevails in the hearing or court case.

Affirm: To uphold the opinion of a lower court on appeal.

Allegation: A claim or assertion made in a hearing or court case by a party who intends to prove it in the hearing or court case.

Alternate assessment based on alternate academic achievement standards (AA-AAAS): State assessments of academic progress for students who cannot participate in regular assessments even with accommodations. Such students are tested using an alternate assessment based on alternate academic achievement standards (AA-AAAS). The Every Student Succeeds Act requires that only students with the most significant cognitive disabilities may take an AA-AAAS.

Alternative dispute resolution: Procedures for settling disputes by means other than litigation—for example, by arbitration or mediation. Such procedures are usually less costly and faster.

Americans with Disabilities Act (ADA): A civil rights law that prohibits discrimination against individuals with disabilities in all areas of public life, including jobs, schools, transportation, and all public and private places open to the public.

Appeal: A party's request to a higher court to review a decision by a lower court. In cases where the right exists, the appeal must be made according to certain procedures and limitations.

Appellant: The party bringing a court appeal.

Appellate court: Any state or federal court empowered to review and amend the judgments of a lower court over which it has jurisdiction.

Appellee: The party responding and defending against the appeal.

Arbitrary: Without rational basis, underlying reason, or guiding principle; nonrational, capricious.

Attention Deficit Hyperactivity Disorder (ADHD): A common disorder of childhood involving inattention, impulsivity, and hyperactivity. Attention deficit hyperactivity disorder often lasts into adulthood.

Average per-pupil expenditure (APPE): The average per-pupil expenditure is the average amount of funds spent per student. This amount varies by state and by districts within a state.

Behavior Intervention Plan (BIP): A behavior intervention plan (BIP) is an individual plan for addressing a student's behaviors. It may be part of a student's IEP but is sometimes a separate document. A BIP is based on the results of an FBA and includes a description of the problem behavior, why the problem behavior occurs, and intervention strategies that include positive behavioral supports and interventions.

Case law: A primary source of law or legal authority formed by the body of reported court cases.

Cert. Denied: The abbreviation used in legal citations to indicate the Supreme Court denied a petition for writ of certiorari in the case being cited.

Certiorari: Abbreviated as cert., a certiorari is a petition for a superior court to review the decision of a lower court. Review may be granted or denied at the discretion of the superior court.

CFR: Abbreviation for Code of Federal Regulations—the repository regulations promulgated by various federal agencies in order to implement laws passed by Congress.

Citation: In legal writing, a notation that directs the reader to a specific source of authority such as a court case, statute, regulation, or journal article.

Civil action: A lawsuit, as opposed to a criminal prosecution, commenced in order to recover a private or civil right or to obtain a remedy for the violation of such a right.

Civil rights or civil liberties: Personal rights guaranteed and protected by the Constitution or state constitutions—for example, freedom of speech and the press, freedom from discrimination.

Class action: A lawsuit brought by one or more members of an ascertainable class who sue on behalf of themselves and others in the larger group who have the same complaint and seek the same remedy.

Code: A written collection of laws or regulations arranged according to an elaborate subject-matter classification scheme (e.g., the US Code and the Code of Federal Regulations).

Color of law: Generally, the semblance, without the substance, of legal right; misuse of power made possible because the wrongdoer is clothed with the authority of the state.

Common law: Law deriving its authority not from legislative enactments, but from ancient and continuing custom or from the judgments and decrees of courts enforcing those customs.

Compensatory damages: A judicial award intended to compensate a plaintiff for an actual loss.

Complaint: The original pleading that initiates a lawsuit and that sets forth a claim for relief.

Complaint resolution process (CRP): States must have a procedure for resolving complaints regarding special education issues. A student's parents or another agency may file a complaint against a school district. If the state agency determines an investigation is warranted, the state may conduct an on-site investigation and issue a written decision. If the state finds the school district failed to provide appropriate services to a student, the decision may include remedies and corrective actions the school district must take.

Consent decree: An order of a judge based on an agreement between the parties in a lawsuit. In such situations the parties will not continue the case in a hearing or trial.

Damages: The monetary compensation awarded by a court to the prevailing party in a lawsuit for injury, loss, or other harm done to their rights, their property, or their person through the illegal or wrongful conduct of another.

Dear Colleague Letter (DCL): Executive agencies in the government often write open letters addressed to "Dear Colleague" in order to announce policy interpretations of federal law and to disseminate this information to the public.

Declaratory relief: A judgment or opinion of the court that merely sets forth the rights of the parties without ordering anything to be done.

Defendant: The defending party in a civil action who must answer the complaint, the plaintiff's opponent.

De novo: A trial *de novo* refers to a situation where a court hears evidence and testimony that may have been previously heard by a lower court or administrative body.

Dictum (pl. dicta): Any statement in a judge's opinion that is not essential to the determination of the case; conclusions on which the decision does not turn. Dictum, unlike the holding, is not binding in subsequent cases.

Dissenting opinion: A court opinion, written by a judge or minority of the judges sitting on a court, setting forth views that contradict and often criticize the judgment and reasoning of the majority opinion. Only the majority opinion has the force of law.

Due process hearing (DPH): A due process hearing is an administrative hearing in which a complaint is filed about some aspect of an IDEA–eligible student's identification (or a student thought to be eligible), evaluation, educational placement, or the provision of FAPE to the student. An impartial hearing officer conducts the hearing, hears testimony, and issue a ruling. The decision is final unless the losing party appeals. Most states have a one-tier system for due process hearings in which the state department of education conducts the hearing and the losing party can appeal to state or federal court. A few states have a two-tier system in which the hearing is conducted by a school district or representative appointed by the SEA. The losing party may appeal to the state department of education. A state review officer or panel of review officers will then be appointed to rule on the appeal. After the review officer or panel issues the decision, the losing party may appeal to state or federal court.

Due process of law: A phrase from the Fifth and Fourteenth Amendments of the United States Constitution that generally refers to the reasonable, fair, and equitable application and administration of the law. Procedural due process refers to constitutionally guaranteed rights to fair notice, fair hearing, and other fair procedures in any legal proceedings that might jeopardize one's life, liberty, or property.

Early intervening services (EIS): A school district may use up to 15 percent of its IDEA, Part B funds to implement coordinated early intervening services, which may include programming for students from kindergarten through grade twelve (emphasis on kindergarten through grade three) who have not been identified as needing special education or related services but who need additional academic and behavioral support to succeed in a general education environment.

En banc: An en banc session is a session in which a case is heard before all the judges of a court rather than by one judge or a panel of judges selected from them.

Enjoin: To command, especially a court's command or order forbidding certain action; the word also can mean to require certain action.

Et. seq.: This is generally used in a citation to indicate "and the sections that follow."

Ex parte: An action initiated at the request of one party and without notice to the other party.

Family Education Rights and Privacy Act (FERPA): A federal law passed in 1974 that protects the privacy of students' educational records. The act also gives parents rights to access their children's educational records.

Federal Appendix (Fed. App'x): A publication of Thomson/West in which rulings of the US Court of Appeals that have not been selected for publication in the *Federal Reporter* are published. These cases do not generate binding precedent but may be persuasive.

Federal Register (Fed. Reg.): The official publication of the federal government that contains government agency rules, proposed rules, and public notices. It is published daily.

Federal Reporter (currently F.3d): Decisions of the US courts of appeals for the various circuits selected for publication. The *Federal Reporter* is now in the third series, which is cited as F.3d. Published circuit court decisions are binding precedent in the district courts in that circuit. Unpublished cases may have persuasive authority.

Federal Supplement (currently F. Supp. 3d): A case law reporter of selected opinions from the US district courts published by Thomson/West Publishing. Few of the cases at this level are published and none have binding precedent, but courts nonetheless may consider them persuasive (although published cases are considered more persuasive). The *Federal Supplement* is now in its third series.

Finding: A conclusion or decision upon a question of fact reached because of a judicial examination or an investigation by a court or jury.

Free Appropriate Public Education (FAPE): Public schools are legally obligated to provide a free appropriate public education (FAPE) to IDEA–eligible students. What constitutes a FAPE has been the subject of two rulings of the US Supreme Court: *Board of Education of the Hendrick Hudson Central School District v. Rowley* (1982) and *Andrew F. v. Douglas County School District* (2017).

Functional Behavioral Assessment (FBA): An assessment used to determine the cause or function of a student's behavior. The results of an FBA are usually used to develop a BIP for the student.

Good faith: A term referring to a party's honest intent. A good faith undertaking is one devoid of any fraud or any motive to take unfair advantage. Bad faith is the opposite.

Hearing: A proceeding with definite issues of fact or law to be resolved in which witnesses are heard, the parties confront each other, and an impartial officer presides.

Holding: Part of the court's decision that applies the law to the facts of the case.

Impartial hearing officer (IHO): An impartial third-party decision maker who conducts an administrative hearing and renders a decision on the merits of the dispute.

Independent educational evaluation (IEE): An independent educational evaluation (IEE) is conducted by a qualified person who is not employed by a school district. An IEE, whether obtained by parents at their own expense or obtained and paid for by a school district, must be considered by a student's IEP team.

Individualized education program (IEP): An individualized education program (IEP) is a program of special education and related services for a student developed by a school-based team in collaboration with the student's parents. An IEP is the embodiment of a student's FAPE.

Individualized family services plan (IFSP): An individualized family services plan (IFSP) is a plan developed for children who are eligible for early intervention services under Part C of the IDEA. A child's IFSP is developed by a team of specialists and the child's parents. It involves the child and his or her family.

Individuals with Disabilities Education Act (IDEA): A federal law, originally the Education for All Handicapped Children Act, passed in 1975 that guarantees an FAPE to eligible students with disabilities

Injunction: An equitable remedy or court order forbidding a party from taking a considered action, restraining the party from continuing an action, or requiring a party to take some action.

In re: In the matter of.

Judgment: The decision of a court that has the authority to resolve the dispute.

Jurisdiction: Legal right by which a court exercises its authority; this also refers to the geographic area within which a court has the authority to rule.

Local educational agency (LEA): A public school district in a state.

Maintenance of effort (MOE): The maintenance of effort (MOE) requirement of IDEA obligates any school district receiving IDEA Part B funds to budget and spend at least the same amount of local or state and local funds for the education of children with disabilities on a year-to-year basis.

Maintenance of state financial support (MFS): Under Part B of the IDEA states are required to make available at least the same amount of state financial support from one year to the next for the education of children with disabilities. This MFS requirement includes reporting obligations.

Moot: When a real or live controversy no longer exists; a legal suit becomes moot if, for example, there is no longer any dispute because a student with a disability turns twenty-one years old.

Multitiered system of support (MTSS): A schoolwide multitiered system of support (MTSS) is a data-driven, problem-solving framework to improve outcomes for all students. An MTSS relies on a continuum of evidence-based practices matched to student needs. The philosophy behind an MTSS is that students at risk for developing academic or behavior problems will receive interventions in order to prevent the development of these problems.

Office of Civil Rights (OCR): The Office of Civil Rights (OCR) is an office within the US Department of Education responsible for ensuring equal access to education through the enforcement of civil rights laws. The laws enforced by the OCR prohibit discrimination based on race, color, national origin, sex, disability, and age in programs that receive federal financial assistance. In the disability area OCR is specifically responsible for enforcing Section 504 of the Rehabilitation Act of 1973 and Title II of the Americans with Disabilities Act.

Office of Special Education and Rehabilitative Services (OSERS): The Office of Special Education and Rehabilitative Service (OSERS) is an office within the US Department of Education. The OSERS was originally established as the Bureau of Education for the Handicapped (BEH) in the Department of Health, Education, and Welfare (HEW). In 1980, when the HEW was divided into two separate departments—the Department of Health and Human Services and the Department of Education—the BEH became the OSERS. The mission of the OSERS is to provide leadership in order to ensure access and excellence in education, independent living, employment, and community living.

Office of Special Education Programs (OSEP): The Office of Special Education Programs (OSEP) is an office within the OSERS. It primarily provides leadership, information, and financial support to states on policies related to the IDEA. The OSEP also provides grants to institutions of higher education.

On remand: This occurs when a higher court returns a case to a lower court with directions that the lower court is to take further action.

Part B: The section of the IDEA that lays out the educational guidelines for schoolchildren between three and twenty-one years of age.

Part C: Part C of the IDEA is a federal grant program that assists states in operating a comprehensive statewide program of early intervention services for infants and toddlers ages birth through two years with disabilities and their families.

Per curiam: Literally, "for or by the court." An unsigned decision of the court as opposed to one signed by a specific judge.

Petition for writ of certiorari: A document a losing party files with the Supreme Court asking that court to review the decision of a lower court.

Petitioner: The party who presents a petition to the court.

Plaintiff: The party who brings suit in a court of law by filing a complaint.

Precedent: Any decided case that may be used as authority in deciding subsequent similar cases.

Preponderance of the evidence: Level of legal proof required in a civil suit; evidence that has greater weight is more convincing. Conversely, a criminal case requires proof beyond a reasonable doubt.

Privacy, right of: The right to live without unwarranted interference by the public in matters with which the public is not necessarily concerned; the right of a person to be free from unwarranted publicity. The term encompasses several rights recognized as inherent in the concept of "ordered liberty." This right is not absolute.

Pro se: This refers to a person who represents himself or herself in a court of law.

Public law (P.L.): A public law is a statute passed by Congress. The IDEA was initially referred to as P.L. 94-142, the 142nd piece of legislation signed by the president during the 94th Congress.

Punitive damages: Compensation awarded to a plaintiff that is over and above the actual loss suffered; these damages are designed to punish the defendant for wrongful action and to act as an incentive to prevent similar action in the future. Courts have determined that punitive damages are not available under the IDEA.

Reevaluation: A complete and thorough reassessment of a student. Generally, all of the original assessments will be repeated, but additional assessments must be completed if necessary; the IDEA 2004 requires educators to reevaluate each child with a disability at least every three years.

Remand: To return a legal case to a lower court, usually with specific instructions for further action.

***Res judicata*:** Meaning "a thing decided." A rule that a final judgment of a court is conclusive and acts to prevent subsequent action on the same legal claim.

Respondent: The party against whom a petition is filed, especially one on appeal. The respondent can be either the plaintiff or the defendant from the court below, as either party can appeal the decision thereby making themselves the petitioner and their adversary the respondent.

Response to intervention (RTI): Response to intervention (RTI) is a schoolwide multitiered framework in which students with learning and behavior needs are identified and receive support. In an RTI system struggling learners are provided with interventions at increasing levels of intensity to match their individual needs.

Section 504: Section 504 of the Rehabilitation Act of 1973 guarantees certain rights to people with disabilities. No otherwise qualified individual with a disability in the United States shall, solely by reason of her or his disability, be excluded from the participation in, be denied the benefits of, or be subjected to discrimination under any program or activity receiving federal financial aid.

Section 1983: Section 1983, titled the Civil Action for the Deprivation of Rights, provides a person the right to sue state government employees and others acting under color of state law for constitutional violations, civil rights violations, or violations of other federal laws.

Settlement agreement: An out-of-court agreement made by the parties to a lawsuit in order to settle the case by resolving the major issues that initiated the litigation.

Standing: An individual's right to bring a suit to court: to have standing an individual must be directly affected by and have a real interest in the issues litigated.

***Stare decisis*:** Meaning "let the decision stand." This refers to following a legal precedent.

State educational agency (SEA): The agency within a state's governing structure responsible for overseeing public education in that state.

State review officer (SRO): An impartial person or sometimes a panel of usually three or more people who reviews the decisions of an independent hearing officer from an administrative due process proceeding under the IDEA. The IDEA provides that if administrative due process hearings are held at the local school district level, provisions must be made for an appeal at the state level.

Statute of limitations: Specifies the period of time within which a legal suit must be filed.

Sua sponte: A Latin phrase that means "of his, her, its, or their own accord." The phrase refers to actions by a court when it takes an action not based on a request made by another party.

Summary judgement: A judgment entered by a court for one party and against another party without a full trial. Summary judgments may be issued on the merits of an entire case or on a single issue in that case.

Title 1 of the Elementary and Secondary Act (Title 1): Now titled the Every Student Succeeds Act, Title 1 is the largest federal aid program for public schools in the United States. The funds pay for extra educational services that help at-risk students achieve and succeed regardless of any disadvantages they face through no fault of their own.

Tuition reimbursement: When a school district reimburses a student's parents for the tuition expenses of a private school placement. This usually occurs when the student's parents unilaterally place their child in a private school and succeed when they seek tuition reimbursement in a due process hearing.

United States Code (USC): The official compilation of statutes enacted by Congress.

US DOE: This is the official abbreviation of the US Department of Energy. This abbreviation is often used incorrectly as an abbreviation of the US Department of Education.

US ED: The official abbreviation of the US Department of Education.

Vacate: Set aside a lower court's decision in an appeal.

Writ of certiorari: A decision by the Supreme Court to hear an appeal from a lower court.

References

Board of Education of the Hendrick Hudson Central School District v. *Rowley*, 458 U.S. 162 (1982).
Endrew F. v. *Douglas County School District RE-1*, 137 S. Ct. 988 (2018).
Fry v. *Napoleon Community Schools,* 137 S. Ct. 743 (2017).
Individuals with Disabilities Education Act (IDEA), 20 U.S.C. § 1400 et seq.
Individuals with Disabilities Education Act (IDEA) Regulations, 34 C.F.R. § 300 et seq.
Office of Civil Rights (OCR), https://www2.ed.gov/about/offices/list/ocr/index.html.
Office of Special Education and Rehabilitative Services (OSERS), https://www2.ed.gov/about/offices/list/osers/index.html.
Office of Special Education Programs (OSEP), https://www2.ed.gov/about/offices/list/osers/osep/index.html#:~:text=The%20Office%20of%20Special%20Education,assist%20states%20and%20local%20districts.
Paul G. v. *Monterey Peninsula Unified School District*, 933 F.3d 1096 (9th Cir. 2019).
R.S. v. *Board of Directors of Woods Charter School Company*, 919 F.3d 237 (4th Cir. 2020).
Yell, M.L. (2019). *The law and special education* (5th ed.). Pearson.
Zirkel, P.A. (2020). Questionable initiation of both dispute resolution processes under the IDEA: Proposed regulatory interpretations. *Journal of Law and Education*, 49(1), 99–109.

Index

A

A.A. & K.K. v. NORTHSIDE INDEPENDENT SCHOOL DISTRICT, 113–114
A.B., by and through his parents and natural guardians, F.B. and N.V., of Effort, PA v. PLEASANT VALLEY SCHOOL DISTRICT, 98
abuse and neglect of students, 130–131, 163
administrative review process, exhaustion of, 111–112, 115, 123–125, 138, 142–143, 146, 148–149, 151–152, 158–159
adult special education residential placement guidelines, 154–155
US Court of Appeals rulings on, 106
A.H. v. Austin Independent School District, 111–112
A.L., by and through her guardian, I. LEE v. CLOVIS UNIFIED SCHOOL DISTRICT et al, 138
allowable costs charged to federal awards, OSERS guidelines, 4–5
Alternate Assessment Aligned with Alternate Academic Achievement Standards (AA-AAAS), waivers for SEAs, 23–27
Americans with Disabilities Act (Title I)
administrative review process in, 111–112
COVID-19 guidelines for services to children with disabilities, 12–17, 19–22
online access to, 69–74
overview of, 1
protected activity standard and, 132
A.N., individually and on behalf of R.N., R.N., individually and on behalf of R.N. v. BOARD OF EDUCATION FOR THE IROQUOIS CENTRAL SCHOOL DISTRICT, 88–89
Andrew MOYNIHAN; Karen MOYNIHAN v. WEST CHESTER AREA SCHOOL DISTRICT; PENNSYLVANIA OFFICE FOR DISPUTE RESOLUTION, 99
appeals
in dispute resolution procedures, 63
in US Courts of Appeals, 65–67
athletics/extracurricular activities, disability discrimination and, 127–128
attorney's fees
IDEA provisions on collection of, 166–167
multiple party requests for, 101
payment of, 107–108, 147
reasonableness of, US Court of Appeals ruling on, 98
recovery of, 137
average annual per pupil expenditure (APPE), IDEA Part B excess cost requirements, 47–48

B

Barnett v. Memphis City School System, 294 F. Supp.2d 924, 70
basic minimum education standard, 129
B.B., by and through his parents CATHERINE B. and JIMMY B. of Philadelphia Pennsylvania v. DELAWARE COLLEGE PREPARATORY ACADEMY; DELAWARE DEPARTMENT OF EDUCATION, 100

180 Index

Behavioral Intervention Plan (BIP), 160–161

BELLFLOWER UNIFIED SCHOOL DISTRICT v. Fernando LUA, individually and on behalf of minor K.L., Sandra LUA, individually and on behalf of minor K.L., 139

BENTONVILLE SCHOOL DISTRICT v. Lisa SMITH, as parent of M.S., a minor, 133

blogs on special education, sources for, 73–74

Board of Education of Gallup-McKinley County Schools v. Native American Disability Law Center, 162

Board of Education of the Hendrick Hudson Central School District v. Rowley (1982), 64–65, 71

BOARD OF EDUCATION OF THE WAPPINGERS CENTRAL SCHOOL DISTRICT v. D.M., as the parent of E.M., a student with a disability, A.M., as the parent of E.M., 90

bullying, US Court of Appeals rulings on, 103–104

Bureau of Indian Education (BIE), COVID-19 guidelines for services to children with disabilities, 11–17

Burlington Carter test, 160–161

BUTTE SCHOOL DISTRICT NO. 1 v. C.S.; Stuart MCCARVEL, in his capacity as originator of the C.S. due process complaint, 140–141

C

Centers for Disease Control and Prevention (CDC), COVID-19 guidelines for services to children with disabilities, 11–17

Chad RICHARDSON, individually, and as parents and next friends of L; Tonya RICHARDSON, individually, and as parents and next friends of L v. OMAHA SCHOOL DISTRICT; Jacob SHERWOOD, superintendent; Amanda GREEN, principal; Dawn DILLON, teacher, 137

Cherryl KIRILENKO-ISON; Susan BAUDER-SMITH v. BOARD OF EDUCATION OF DANVILLE INDEPENDENT SCHOOLS, 132

Child-find requirement (IDEA), 116–117, 121–122

Christopher GLOSTON, by Tamika GLOSTON, his next friend, parent, and natural guardian v. Jack VANCE, 163

Code of Federal Regulations (CFR), 70

comparable services principle, IEPs and, 109–110

compensatory education, 133
as FAPE remedy, 116–117

complaint resolution process (CRP)
dispute resolution using, 61–62
parents' First Amendment rights and, 150
state education agencies, 61–62

confidentiality agreement, OSERS guidelines, 8–10

continuity of services, funding for, IDEA Part C guidelines, 43

Cost Principles of Uniform Guidance, 4–5

COVID-19
dispute resolution procedures during, 28–31
education programs and, xi–xii
services to children with disabilities during, 11–17
Supplemental Fact Sheet, 18–22

Cynthia SORIA, individually and as parent and natural guardian of G.S., Giovanni SORIA, individually and as parent and natural guardian of G.S. v. NEW YORK CITY DEPARTMENT OF EDUCATION, 96

Cypress-Fairbanks Independent School District v. Michael F., 114, 120

Index

D

Daniel R. R. v. State Board of Education (1989), 67
D.D., a minor, by and through his guardian ad litem, Michaela INGRAM v. LOS ANGELES UNIFIED SCHOOL DISTRICT, 142–143
Dear Colleague Letter
  examples of, 4–9
  purpose of, 1–2
denial of access, litigation involving, 142–143
de novo hearings, special education disputes, 65
different treatment principle, FAPE and, 132
disability discrimination, 127–128
  determination of, 157
  student abuse and neglect, 130–131, 163
  student complaints of, 151–152
discrimination based on disability, 127–128
dispute resolution procedures
  federal court system, 63–68
  IDEA Part B guidelines for, 28–31, 61–68
  IDEA Part C guidelines for, 32–35
  jurisdictional issues, 99
  published and unpublished decisions, 68
  rejection of settlement, 107–108
  state education agencies, 61–62
  in US Courts of Appeals, 65–67
  in US District Courts, 63–65
  US Supreme Court and, 67–68
distance learning plans, COVID-19 guidelines for services to children with disabilities, 14–15, 19–22
D.L., by next friend Frances LANDON, by next friend MollyJayne LANDON v. ST. LOUIS CITY SCHOOL DISTRICT, 134
Doe v. Harlandale Independent School District, 115
Donahue v. Kansas Board of Education, 158–159
D.S., by and through his parents and next friends, M.S. and R.S. v. TRUMBULL BOARD OF EDUCATION, 91
due process hearing (DPH)
  administrative review process and, 115
  COVID-19 timeline extensions, 29–31, 33–35
  IDEA impartiality guidelines, 6–7
  IDEA timeline for, 21–22, 100
  overview, 62–63
  pro se procedures, 158–159
  published and unpublished decisions, 68
  in US Courts of Appeals, 65–67
  in US District Courts, 64–65
  US Supreme Court and, 68
  virtual meetings for, 31

E

Early Childhood Technical Assistance Center (ECTA), 20
early intervening services (EIS)
  COVID-19 guidelines for services to children with disabilities, 11–12, 15–17
  dispute resolution procedures, IDEA Part C, 32–35
  funding for, IDEA Part C guidelines, 42–44
  IDEA Part C procedural safeguards and, 53–56
  initial evaluation timeline requirements, IDEA Part C, 58–60
early testing windows, AAAAAS One Percent Cap, waiver requirements, 26–27
education records access
  adult special education students, 106
  early intervention records, IDEA Part C procedural safeguards, 55–56
  IDEA Part B provisions concerning, 52
  non-residential student services and, 105

electronic/digital copies
　early intervention records, IDEA Part C procedural safeguards, 55–56
　IDEA Part B provisions concerning, 51–52
electronic/digital signatures
　IDEA Part B provisions for, 49–52
　IDEA Part C provisions for, 54–56
Elementary and Secondary Education Act of 1965 (ESEA) (Title I), AAAAAS One Percent Cap requirements, 24–27
eligibility guidelines, US Court of Appeals rulings on, 135
Elizabeth B. v. El Paso County School District 11, 160–161
En banc hearings, special education disputes, 67
Endrew F. v. Douglas County School District, 113–114, xi
enrollment guidelines for special education, 156
equipment expenditures
　IDEA Part B funds for, 38–40
　IDEA Part C funds for, 43–44
escrow accounts, IDEA provisions concerning, US Appeals Court review of, 92
Esther DE LA FUENTE, on her own behalf and on behalf of A.D. v. ROOSEVELT ELEMENTARY SCHOOL DISTRICT NO. 66, a political subdivision of the State of Arizona; Jeanne N. KOBA, an individual; Jonathan MOORE, an individual; Freddy MONTOYA, an individual; Cynthia BERNACKI, an individual, and Brent RUSSELL, an individual; KELLY SERVICES, INC., a foreign corporation, 144
EVERETT H. et al. v. DRY CREEK JOINT ELEMENTARY SCHOOL DISTRICT et al., 145

exceptional circumstances exception
　dispute resolution procedures, COVID-19 guidelines, 29
　initial evaluation timeline requirements, IDEA Part C, 58–60
excess cost requirements, IDEA Part B provisions, 47–48

F

Family Educational Rights and Privacy Act (FERPA), 54
Federal Appendix, 68
federal court system
　jurisdictional issues, 99
　special education disputes in, 63–68
Federal Reporter, 68, 70
FindLaw website, 71–74
First Amendment, parents' rights under, 150
fiscal requirements, IDEA provisions, Part B provisions, 45–48
four-factor FAPE test, 114, 120
Free Appropriate Public Education (FAPE)
　COVID-19 guidelines for services to children with disabilities, 12–17, 19–22, xi–xii
　different treatment principle and, 132
　dispute resolution procedures involving, 63
　IEPs and standard for, 103–104, 118–122
　procedural violations of, 158–159
　school district obligations concerning, 139, 153
　US Court of Appeals rulings on, 103–104
　violations of, 113–114, 116–117, 121–122
Fry v. Napoleon Community Schools, 123–125, 152

Index **183**

functional behavioral assessments (FBAs) procedures for, 160–161
US District Court review of, 91
funds guidelines
   IDEA Part B guidelines, 36–40
   IDEA Part C guidelines, 41–44
   trust funds and escrow accounts, IDEA provisions, 92

G

GARY B., JESSIE K., CRISTOPHER R., ISAIAS R., ESMERALDA V., PAUL M., and JAIME R., minors, plaintiffs v. Gretchen WHITMER et al., 129
G.B., a minor, by and through his parents by next friend Nancy A. BARBOUR by next friend Cynthia L. NONEMACHER, Nancy A. BARBOUR, parent and next friend to G.B., a minor, Cynthia L. NONEMACHER, parent and next friend to G.B., a minor v. ORANGE SOUTHWEST SUPERVISORY DISTRICT, 93
Google Scholar website, 71–74

H

harassment/retaliation
   against school nurses, 132
   against special education teachers, 95

I

I.K., on behalf of Z.S. v. MONTCLAIR BOARD OF EDUCATION, 101
impartial hearing officer (IHO)
   dispute resolution procedures, 63
   US District Court appeal of decisions by, 64–65
independent educational evaluation (IEE) school district obligations concerning, 140–141
   US District Court reivew of, 91
INDEPENDENT SCHOOL DISTRICT NO. 283 v. E.M.D.H., a minor, by and through her parents and next friends, L.H. and S.D., 135
individualized education program (IEP)
   AAAAAS One Percent Cap requirements, 24–27
   comparable services principle and, 109–110
   COVID-19 guidelines for services to children with disabilities, 13–15, 19–22
   IDEA Part B funds for, 39–40
   IDEA timeline for, 21
   LEA review of, 139
   necessary components of, 153
   student placement guidelines, 134
   US Court of Appeals rulings on, 103–104, 118–120, 133
individualized family service plan (IFSP)
   COVID-19 guidelines for services to children with disabilities, 15–17
   IDEA Part C funds for, 43–44
   IDEA timeline for, 22
   initial evaluation timeline requirements, IDEA Part C, 58–60
   interim IFSP, IDEA Part C provisions for, 59–60
Individuals with Disabilities Act (IDEA)
   AAAAAS One Percent Cap requirements, 23–27
   administrative review procedures, 111–112, 115
   attorney's fees guidelines, 166–167
   child-find requirement, 116–117, 121–122
   confidentiality agreement guidelines, 8–10
   COVID-19 guidelines for services to children with disabilities, 11–17, 19–22, xi–xii
   COVID-19-related timeline extensions under, 29–31, 33–35
   dispute resolution procedures (Part B), 28–31, 61–68

184 Index

Individuals with Disabilities Act (*Continued*)
dispute resolution procedures (Part C), 32–35
eligibility guidelines, 135
fiscal requirements, Part B provisions, 45–48, 92
funds applications, Part B guidelines, 36–40, 92
impartial due process hearing guidelines, 6–7
initial evaluation and assessment timeline, Part C requirements, 57–60
noncustodial parents legal standing under, 126
online access to, 69–74
overview, 1
Part B implementation during COVID-19 outbreak, 12–15, 20–22
Part C implementation during COVID-19 outbreak, 15–17, 20, 22
private school tuition reimbursement under, 88–89, 102–103
procedural safeguards, Part B provisions, 49–52
remedies for violations of, 109–110
stay-put provisions in, 94, 96–97
student placement guidelines, 134
timelines, 20–22
transportation entitlements under, 136
initial eligibility determination
IDEA Part B timeline for, 21
IDEA Part C timeline for, 57–60
US Court of Appeals review of, 91
interim individualized family service plan (IFSP), IDEA Part C provisions for, 59–60

J

Jane DOE, John DOE, by and through his parent Jane DOE, plaintiffs-appellants v. EAST LYME BOARD OF EDUCATION, CONNECTICUT STATE DEPARTMENT OF EDUCATION, 92
Jennifer GARZA, individually and as guardian ad litem for C.G. on behalf of C.G. v. LANSING SCHOOL DISTRICT; Connie NICKSON; Tracey KEATON; Martin ALWARDT; Yvonne CAAMAL CANUL; Sheryl BACON; Edna ROBINSON, 130–131
J.F., a minor, by and through guardians ad litem Aron FEILES and Alexandra FEILES, individually on and on behalf of the proposed class v. SAN DIEGO UNIFIED SCHOOL DISTRICT, a government entity, 146
J.F. and J.F., on behalf of J.F. v. BYRAM TOWNSHIP BOARD OF EDUCATION, 102
J.M.; Marla McDONALD v. OAKLAND UNIFIED SCHOOL DISTRICT, 147
J.T. v. DISTRICT OF COLUMBIA, 168
jurisdictional issues, special education disputes, 99
Justia website, 71–74

K

K.D., a minor, by and through her guardian ad litem, Leila CARERRA v. LOS ANGELES UNIFIED SCHOOL DISTRICT, 148–149
K.E.; B.E., on behalf of T.E. v. NORTHERN HIGHLANDS REGIONAL BOARD OF EDUCATION, 103–104
Keith Allen, et al. v. DISTRICT OF COLUMBIA, 166–167
Keshia CLEMONS, as mother and next friend of T.W. v. SHELBY COUNTY BOARD OF EDUCATION; Scott

RICKE; John LEEPER; James NIEHOF, superintendent, 127–128
K.K.-M., individually and as kinship legal guardian of the minor children R.M. and A.W. v. NEW JERSEY DEPARTMENT OF EDUCATION; NEW JERSEY OFFICE OF ADMINISTRATIVE LAW; Dominic ROTA; GLOUCESTER CITY BOARD OF EDUCATION, doing business as Gloucester City Public Schools, 105
KOSHK standard, 122

L

least restrictive environment standard, 157
Legal Information Institute (LII) (Cornell Law), 72
Lexyington McINTYRE v. EUGENE SCHOOL DISTRICT 4J, and Cheryl LINDER; Andy DEY; Michael STASACK; Susie NICHOLSON; Suzie McLAUCHLIN, 151–152
L.F., in his individual capacity and as parent of K.S.F (Student 1) and K.S.F. (Student 2); K.S.F., Student 1; K.S.F., Student 2 v. LAKE WASHINGTON SCHOOL DISTRICT #414, 150
literacy, right to, 129
local educational agency (LEA)
 AAAAAS One Percent Cap, waiver requirements, 25–27
 COVID-19 guidelines for services to children with disabilities, 11–17
 dispute resolution procedures, IDEA Part B guidelines, 28–31, 61–63
 dispute resolution procedures, IDEA Part C guidelines, 32–35
 due process hearings timeline, 21–22, 29–31, 33–35
 FAPE obligations of, 139
 fiscal requirements, IDEA Part B, 46–48
 funding applications, IDEA Part B guidelines, 36–40
 funding applications, IDEA Part C guidelines, 41–44
 IDEA impartiality guidelines for, 6–7
L.W. v. JERSEY CITY BOARD OF EDUCATION; the PARSIPPANY-TROY HILLS BOARD OF EDUCATION, 106

M

maintenance of effort (MOE) requirements, IDEA Part B provisions, 46–48
Maintenance of State financial support (MFS), fiscal requirements, IDEA Part B, 45–46
mediation procedures, COVID-19 timelines, 30–31, 33–35
medical complications, COVID-19 guidelines for services to children with, 13–14
medical records, evaluation and assessment using, IDEA Part C guidelines, 59–60
Michele PISTELLO v. BOARD OF EDUCATION OF THE CANASTOTA CENTRAL SCHOOL DISTRICT, 95
moot cases, US Appeals Court determination of, 99, 133, 145, 168

N

NESKE, individually and as parent and natural guardian of A.N. v. NEW YORK CITY DEPARTMENT OF EDUCATION, 94
N.G., a conserved adult, by and through her conservators, R.G. and G.G. et al. v. PLACENTIA YORBA LINDA UNIFIED SCHOOL DISTRICT, 154–155
noncustodial parents, legal standing of, 126

nonresidential students
  special education services for, 105
  transportation entitlements for, 136

O

Office of Civil Rights (OCR)
  COVID-19 Supplemental Fact Sheet, 18–22
  policy statements, 1–2
Office of Special Education and Related Services (OSERS)
  confidentiality agreement guidelines, 8–10
  Dear Colleague letters, 4–9
  policy statements, 1–2
  Supplemental Fact Sheet on COVID-19, 18–22
Office of Special Education Programs (OSEP)
  confidentiality agreement guidelines, 8–10
  dispute resolution procedures, COVID-19 guidelines, 28–31
  policy statements, 1–2
Okwuldi Francis CHUKWUANI, M.D. v. SOLON CITY SCHOOL DISTRICT, 126
online special education legal resources, 69–74
OSSEO AREA SCHOOLS, INDEPENDENT SCHOOL DISTRICT NO. 279 v. M.N.B., by and through her parent, J.B., 136

P

paraprofessional services, guidelines for, 153
parental involvement in special education
  access to education records, IDEA Part B provisions concerning, 52
  documentation of denial of, 140–141
  IDEA Part B provisions, 49–52
  IDEA Part C provisions, 53–56
  importance of, 164–165

Parents' First Amendment rights, 150
personally identifiable information (PII)
  IDEA Part B procedural safeguards for, 50–52
  IDEA Part C procedural safeguards for, 54–56
P.P. v. Northwest Independent School District, 116–117
prior written notice requirements
  IDEA Part B procedural safeguards, 51–52
  IDEA Part C procedural safeguards, 55–56
private school
  appropriate placement in, 139
  tuition reimbursement for, 88–90, 102–103
procedural safeguards
  FAPE violations and, 158–159, 164–165
  IDEA Part B provisions, 49–52
  IDEA Part C provisions, 53–56
  parental involvement and, 164–165
  school district obligations concerning, 140–141
pro se procedures for DPH, 158–159
protected activity standard, 132
Public Access to Court Electronic Records (PACER) website, 72

R

reasonable time
  IDEA Part B procedural safeguards, 51–52
  IDEA Part C procedural safeguards, 55
reevaluations, IDEA timeline for, 22
Regina Marie PANGERL, individually and on behalf of T.P. v. PEORIA UNIFIED SCHOOL DISTRICT, 156
Rehabilitation Act Section 504. *See* Section 504 (Rehabilitation Act)
rejection of dispute settlement, US Court of Appeals rulings on, 107–108

Index **187**

remote learning platforms, IDEA Part B funds for, 38–40
RENA C., individually and on behalf of A.D. v. COLONIAL SCHOOL DISTRICT, 107
residential placement guidelines, 154–155
R.S. v. BOARD OF DIRECTORS OF WOODS CHARTER SCHOOL COMPANY, 109–110
R.S. v. Board of Directors of Woods Charter School Company, 2020, 67
R.S. v. Highland Park Independent School District, 118–120

S

Sanchez & Z.B. v. DISTRICT OF COLUMBIA PUBLIC SCHOOLS, 164–165
SAVE ACCESS ACADEMY, an unincorporated association v. MULTNOMAH COUNTY SCHOOL DISTRICT NO. 1J, an Oregon public corporate entity by and through the Board of Directors of Multnomah County School District No. 1J; Guadalupe GUERRERO, Superintendent, individually and in his official capacity, 157
school closures, COVID-19 guidelines for services to children with disabilities during, 13
school nurses, harassment and/or retaliation of, 132
Section 504 (Rehabilitation Act)
  administrative review process in, 111–112
  appropriateness of plans in, 146, 148–149, 151–152
  COVID-19 guidelines for services to children with disabilities, 12–17, 19–22
  COVID-19 pandemic impact on, xi–xii
  dispute resolution procedures, 62–63
  online access to, 69–74
  protected activity standard and, 132
  statute of limitations for implementation, 144
special education law, online resources for, 69–74
Spring Branch Independent School District v. O.W., 961 F.3d 781 (5th Cir. 2020), 70, 121–122
state educational agencies (SEA)
  AAAAAS One Percent Cap, waiver requirements, 23–27
  complaint resolution procedures, 61–62
  confidentiality agreement guidelines, 8–10
  COVID-19 guidelines for services to children with disabilities, 11–17
  dispute resolution procedures, IDEA Part B, 29–31
  dispute resolution procedures, IDEA Part C, 32–35
  fiscal requirements, IDEA Part B, 45–46
  funding applications, IDEA Part B guidelines, 37–40
  funding applications, IDEA Part C guidelines, 41–44
  IDEA complaint timeline for, 21–22, 29–31, 33–35
  IDEA impartiality guidelines for, 6–7
state laws and regulations, online access to, 72
State Lead Agency (State LA)
  IDEA Part C procedural safeguards and, 53–56
  initial evaluation timeline requirements, IDEA Part C, 58–60
state review officer (SRO)
  in dispute resolution appeals, 63
  US Court of Appeals review of decision by, 90
statute of limitations
  attorney's fees recovery, 137, 162
  Section 504 implementation, 144
  US Court of Appeals rulings on, 100
  US Court of Appeals rulings on IDEA timelines, 93

stay-put provisions, 156
  US Court of Appeals rulings on, 94, 96–97
student abuse and neglect, 130–131, 163
Supreme Court Reporter, 71

T

T.B. v. Northwest Independent School District, 123–125
teachers in special education
  harassment/retaliation against, 95
  student abuse and neglect by, 130–131, 163
telecommunications systems, funding for, IDEA Part C guidelines, 42–44
Terria McKNIGHT v. LYON COUNTY SCHOOL DISTRICT, 153
timelines
  attorney's fees recovery, 137, 162
  COVID-19 extensions of, 29–31, 33–35
  due process hearings, 21–22, 29–31, 33–35
  in IDEA provisions, 21–22
  for IEPs, 21
  for IFSPs, 22
  for initial eligibility determination, 21, 57–60
  for initial evaluation, 58–60
  reasonable time provisions, 51–52, 55
  US Court of Appeals rulings on, 93, 100
transportation entitlements, nonresident students and, 136
Trust funds, IDEA provisions concerning, US Appeals Court review of, 92
tuition reimbursement
  Burlington Carter test for, 160–161
  US Court of Appeals rulings on, 88–89, 102–104

U

Uniform Guidance, OSERS guidelines, 4–5
United States Code, 69
US Courts of Appeals
  DC Circuit case summaries, 87, 164–168
  Eighth Circuit case summaries, 85, 133–137
  Eleventh Circuit case summaries, 87, 163
  Fifth Circuit case summaries, 85, 111–125
  Fourth Circuit case summaries, 84, 109–110
  Ninth Circuit case summaries, 86–87, 138–157
  Second Circuit case summaries, 83–84, 88–97
  Sixth Circuit case summaries, 85, 126–132
  special education disputes, 65–67, 71
  Tenth Circuit case summaries, 87, 158–162
  Third Circuit case summaries, 84, 98–108
  topics covered in 2020 by, 75–81
US Department of Education
  COVID-19 guidelines for services to children with disabilities during, 11–17
  offices of, 1–2
US District Courts, special education disputes in, 63–65
US Supreme Court, special education disputes, 67–68

V

VENTURA DE PAULINO, individually and as parent and natural guardian of R.P. v. NEW YORK CITY DEPARTMENT

OF EDUCATION and NEW YORK STATE EDUCATION DEPARTMENT, Robert BRIGILIO; Maria NAVARRO CARRILLO, as parent and natural guardian of M.G. and individually; Jose GARZON, as parent and natural guardian of M.G. and individually, plaintiffs-appellees v. NEW YORK CITY DEPARTMENT OF EDUCATION, 97

violations of IDEA, remedies and calculation of awards for, 109–110
virtual meetings
    for dispute resolution and mediation procedures, 30–31, 34–35
    funding for, IDEA Part C guidelines, 42–44

Z

Zirkel, P. A., 61–62

www.ingramcontent.com/pod-product-compliance
Lightning Source LLC
Chambersburg PA
CBHW070612170426
43200CB00012B/2673